Other books by Karl Jaspers in English translation

KARL JASPERS

SPINOZA

From *The Great Philosophers: The Original Thinkers*

Edited by Hannah Arendt

Translated by Ralph Manheim

A HARVEST/HBJ BOOK

HBJ

A HELEN AND KURT WOLFF BOOK

HARCOURT BRACE JOVANOVICH

New York and London

Library of Congress Cataloging in Publication Data

Jaspers, Karl, 1883-1969.
Spinoza.

(A Harvest book, HB 290)
"A Helen and Kurt Wolff book."
Previously published as part of v. 2 of the author's
The great philosophers, which is a translation of
Die grossen Philosophen.
Bibliography: p.
1. Spinoza, Benedictus de, 1632-1677.
[B3998.J3713]   199.492   74-4336
ISBN 0-15-684730-2

First Harvest edition 1974
B C D E F G H I J

Acknowledgment is made for permission to use the following:
For the quotations from Benedict de Spinoza: The Chief Works, 2 volumes,
translated by R. H. M. Elwes, Dover Publications, Inc., New York;
Ethics in the W. H. White translation, Hafner Library of Classics
Philosophy Series, Hafner Publishing Company.

CONTENTS

SPINOZA

SPINOZA

I. LIFE AND WORKS

Spinoza (1632–1677) came of a family of Spanish Jews who had been exiled to Portugal. His parents had emigrated to Holland. He grew up in the great tradition of Judeo-Spanish culture. He knew the Jewish philosophers, studied the Hebrew Bible, the Talmud, the commentators, and Spanish literature. At the age of fifteen, he was looked upon as a future light of the Synagogue.

Later he came into conflict with Jewish scholars, stayed away from the synagogue, and at the age of twenty-four was expelled from the Jewish community. Every effort was made to hold him in the orthodox faith, he was offered an annual stipend if he would go to the synagogue even occasionally. Spinoza refused. When a fanatic tried to murder him, he left Amsterdam and took refuge with a friend. The Synagogue pronounced the anathema against him. Since this measure also had civil consequences, Spinoza protested. But the title of the lost work that he wrote in self-defense—"Apology, to justify himself for leaving the Synagogue"—shows that he himself had taken the initiative in the break. His sisters cited the anathema to deprive him of his paternal inheritance. He went to court and established his rights as a Dutchman. But then he voluntarily abandoned the whole inheritance with the exception of a bed. He never uttered a word of complaint about his sisters except at the end, when he left them out of his will: "Their conduct did not deserve it." Quietly and without recriminations he had broken with his family.

With a view to financial independence, he learned to grind lenses, which were a novelty at the time and very much in demand. He became a master of the craft. However, he did not live by it, but was supported by friends. A number of people offered him money. He often refused. But he accepted the help of Simon de Vries, though he declined to be appointed his heir, since by law and nature the inheritance was due to Simon's brother. When after Simon's death his brother wished to give him five hundred guilders a year, Spinoza reduced the sum to three hundred. Jan de Witt had given him a pension of two hundred guilders, attested in writing. When de Witt's heirs showed unwillingness to continue the pension, he brought them de

Witt's promise and renounced his claim. Whereupon they decided to meet their obligation. Spinoza lived very simply. "The cloak does not make the man. Why a costly covering for a worthless thing?" But he did not neglect his person. He was neat and orderly in his dress and domestic arrangements. Spinoza spent money freely on only one thing: he left behind him a choice and valuable library.

After his excommunication Spinoza led a quiet, modest life in rented rooms in various parts of Holland: 1656–60, in a country house between Amsterdam and Ouverkerk; 1660–63, in Rijnsburg near Leiden; 1663–69, in Voorburg near The Hague; and finally in The Hague, first, from 1669 to 1671, boarding with a widow, then, after 1671, in the house of the painter Hendryk van der Speyk, where he kept house for himself. Here he died of tuberculosis in 1677 at the age of forty-five.

Spinoza did not choose his fate but accepted it as inevitable: it meant exclusion from any community of faith, blood, or tradition, and from his own family. Rejected by the Jews, he did not become a Christian. But he was a Dutch citizen, determined to perform the duties and assert the rights of a citizen.

The Dutch state had developed in struggle against Spanish oppression. The moral force behind the Dutch independence movement had not been nationalism, but a striving for political freedom, justified by religious faith. At the time when the state was founded under the leadership of the house of Orange, the paramount consideration had been military strength. Once Dutch independence had been recognized in the Peace of Westphalia (1648) and the new state began to feel secure, military organization and unified leadership ceased to seem all-important. The republican party (the Dutch patriciate, the oligarchical party) triumphed over the house of Orange. For twenty years the republicans under Jan de Witt maintained a regime of peace and prosperity. Military expenditure was reduced, the state was secured by foreign alliances. Unlike the Orange party, which in practice had been extremely intolerant, the republicans stood for true religious freedom. This gratifying state of affairs came to a sudden end when Louis XIV, in alliance with the King of England, invaded Holland. Regarded as a traitor, Jan de Witt was murdered by the mob (1762). The Orange party returned to power, but the republican spirit preserved a considerable influence.

Spinoza participated in politics. The *Theologico-Political Treatise* (1670) is not only a philosophical investigation; it was conceived and published in support of the political aims of his friend Jan de Witt and the republicans. Jan de Witt was dependent on public opinion for his power. It was essential that the spirit of the government should find an echo in the spirit of the population. Freedom of conscience and independence of the state from Church orthodoxy were among the government's fundamental principles. Spinoza's treatise argued in favor of both.

After the murder of de Witt, the republicans (oligarchical party) strove to carry on in his spirit and to restore peace. With the party's knowledge and approval, Spinoza went to the Prince of Condé's headquarters in Utrecht to promote the cause of peace, though it is possible that he had merely been hoodwinked by a courtier who wished to satisfy Condé's supposed desire to speak to the famous Jew. We are told that Spinoza bore himself with remarkable ease and assurance at Condé's court. But he did not succeed in seeing the Prince and returned home empty-handed. The populace regarded him as a spy. Spinoza's landlord was afraid the mob would break into his house. Spinoza replied: "Do not be alarmed. I am innocent, and there are many among the nobles who know perfectly well why I went to Utrecht. As soon as you hear the least disturbance at your door, I shall go out to the people, even if they choose to deal with me as they did with the good de Witt. I am an honest republican, and the welfare of the Republic is my sole concern." Such was Spinoza's conduct as a Dutch citizen.

The Orange party won out. It introduced (according to the classical definition of state forms, which was accepted also by Spinoza) a monarchy as opposed to the aristocracy of the oligarchical party. In a posthumous political treatise, Spinoza outlined the ideal types of monarchy and aristocracy. At the time of his death he was about to investigate the third type, democracy.

Spinoza was a Dutchman, not by descent but by political right. No longer a member of the Jewish community, he had no other source of security than justice in the political existence of his state. As a man left to his own resources, he recognized his human bond with every other man, and for him this human bond was the self-certainty of reason. Spinoza had not chosen to uproot himself, but when this lot was thrust upon him he found new roots in the eternal reason that is accessible to man as man. His thinking became a refuge for rejected individuals, compelled to stand entirely on their own feet, an orientation for every man who seeks independence. He found the self-certainty of reason in philosophy, which illumined and guided his life. When someone, wishing to convert him to the Catholic faith, accused him of regarding his philosophy as the best, he replied: "I do not claim to have found the best philosophy, but I do know that I recognize the true philosophy."

Spinoza's uprootedness could be made good only by the political security of a constitutional state and by personal relations of a purely human kind. Spinoza had numerous friends and acquaintances, and he carried on an extensive correspondence. He was welcome among the Collegiants, an association of nondenominational Christians. He was a lover of philosophical companionship. "It is essential to my happiness that I make every effort to bring it about that many others should have the same insights as I, and that their knowledge and will coincide completely with my knowledge and will." He never forced his teachings on anyone. But what he said carried conviction. And no one could escape the nobility of his personality; even his enemies could not help respecting him. He liked to associate with simple people. When his landlady asked him if she could find salvation in her religion, he replied: "Your religion is good. There is no need to look for another as long as you lead a quiet life in devotion to God." Although he had good friends, he suffered cruel disappointments in his human relationships; he was misunderstood, exploited, forsaken; toward the end Leibniz came to see the remarkable Jew, whom he was later to disavow completely.

It is not easy to put the right interpretation on Spinoza's desire for independence. He wished to think and to live nothing other than the truth, which for him meant: to be in God. This independence, this confidence in his own judgment: this was the godly life. He was not concerned with his own person. This man, who was so entirely himself, was without self-seeking. He was free from pride and violence and seemed never to think of himself. He wished his *Ethics* to appear only after his death and without his name. For the truth is impersonal. It does not matter who first formulated its propositions. He did not claim to *possess* the truth (it is a very different matter with scientists and mathematicians who justifiably claim priority for their achievements as mere achievements).

Spinoza concluded his letters with a seal inscribed with the Latin word *caute*. He was indeed cautious, for he wished to live in peace. He was very careful to whom he communicated his ideas and gave his manuscripts to read. He postponed publication, and most of his work appeared after his death. He had no desire to be a martyr: "I believe that each man should live as he sees fit; and let those who will die for their happiness, if only I may be permitted to live for the truth." Although he had been assured of full freedom, he declined a call to the University of Heidelberg (1673): "I have misgivings," he wrote to the Palatine minister, "about the limits to be imposed on the freedom to philosophize. . . . I do not hesitate because I hope for better fortune, but for love of a tranquillity which I think cannot be preserved in any other way."

Spinoza was neither a solitary eccentric nor an active statesman. He undertook no other occupation than to develop his ideas systematically and set them down on paper. In other respects, he was an independent man, a citizen, a friend, who reacted to the situations of life with natural good sense—and always in an attitude of piety.

His quiet dignity seems to have been as much an innate disposition as the consequence of his philosophy. But a number of anecdotes show that his serenity was not apathy, that his nature was not lukewarm, that he was not lacking in temperament. At the murder of Jan de Witt, he burst into tears. He wrote a handbill addressed to the mob, beginning: *ultimi barbarorum,* and was going to rush out and post it. When his landlord locked him in his room to save him too from being killed, he came to his senses.

Of the portraits that have come down to us, the one in Wolfenbüttel shows the noble Sephardi. But even such a picture can give only an intimation of the nobility and purity of soul to which his life and work bear witness.

Works: In his lifetime he published under his own name only the didactic, mathematically formulated *Principles of Descartes's Philosophy* (1663) and anonymously the *Theologico-Political Treatise* (1670). Immediately after his death, the *Ethics,* the *Political Treatise, On the Improvement of the Understanding, Letters,* and *Compendium of a Hebrew Grammar* appeared in one volume. In 1852, the *Treatise on God and Man and Man's Happiness* was found.

Chronology: From the period before the anathema nothing has come down to us. The oldest document is the *Short Treatise,* found in 1852 (written before September, 1661, probably between 1658 and 1660), the earliest formulation of Spinoza's thinking. Among the oldest works is the unfinished *Treatise on the Improvement of the Understanding,* important for a comprehension of Spinoza's cast of mind. The *Principles of Descartes's Philosophy* was written in 1662–63. The first draft of his main work, the *Ethics,* was written in 1662–65. It contained three books, which later grew to be five. Spinoza worked on the manuscript up to the time of his death. The *Theologico-Political Treatise* was begun in 1665 and published in 1670. Shortly before his death Spinoza wrote the unfinished *Political Treatise.*

II. PHILOSOPHY AND WAY OF LIFE

Philosophy was implicit in Spinoza's life; it was his only means of attaining his goal. In his early work on the *Improvement of the Understanding,* he reflected on his future course. Everything, he reflected, contains good or evil insofar as the soul is affected by it. What life commonly offers proves to be vain and worthless. And so "I finally resolved to inquire whether there might be some real good having power to communicate itself, which would affect the mind singly, to the exclusion of all else; whether, in fact, there might be anything of which the discovery and attainment would enable me to enjoy continuous, supreme, and unending happiness. I say 'I *finally* resolved,' for at first sight it seemed unwise willingly to lose hold on what was sure for the sake of something then uncertain." Riches, fame, the pleasures of sense seem to be certainties. But it is not certain that the highest good is to be found in them. For sensual pleasure results in a confusion and blunting of the mind. Wealth calls for more and more wealth. In search of honor, I must incline to the opinions of men, avoid what they avoid and seek what they seek. If I am to strive in earnest for the new, the truly good, I must renounce all these things. For they are so demanding that the mind preoccupied with them cannot think any other good. Thus my quest for the true good requires me to sacrifice a good that is uncertain by its very nature for a good which is also at first uncertain, but which is not by nature uncertain. In the midst of a life fettered to questionable, perishable goods, which are certain to melt into nothingness, I shall do well to seek salvation along the new path as a remedy, although it too is uncertain.

The first question is: On what do happiness and unhappiness depend? And the answer: On the nature of the objects that we love. There are two kinds of object. In our love of perishable objects and of those which all men cannot acquire in equal measure, we expose ourselves to envy, fear, and hatred. "But love toward a thing eternal and infinite feeds the mind wholly with joy, and is itself unmingled with any sadness." Experience taught Spinoza that though the mind, enlightened by such insight, can turn away from perishable things, it cannot abolish them. His moments of liberation became longer and more frequent, but he became truly free only after he had gained a second insight, namely, that the acquisition of money, the pleasures of the senses, and honors, are harmful only as long as they are pursued as ends in themselves. For once they are treated as means, they are moderated and cease to be harmful. This attitude of natural moderation is characteristic of Spinoza. His highest good does not destroy everything else. It is not to be expected in the beyond, but to be seized upon and fulfilled in this world.

What is this highest good? In his youth Spinoza stated the answer briefly: insight into the unity which binds the human spirit to all nature and enables me, in community with other men, to participate in nature. Whatever comes my way should be considered as a means to this end; I should concern myself with it only insofar as it is necessary as a means. From this certain conclusions can be drawn:

We must understand as much of nature as is necessary in order to bring about the highest possible nature in man.

We must establish the kind of society that is necessary if many men are to attain this end as easily and surely as possible.

We must find an ethical philosophy and a doctrine of education leading in this direction.

We must promote medicine for the sake of men's health, which is far from negligible as a means to our end.

We must improve mechanics in order to make difficult things easy, so saving much time and trouble.

We must find means to purify the understanding, in order that it may know things readily, without error, and as completely as possible.

Thus all the sciences should be oriented toward a single aim, which is the highest human perfection.

Provisional rules for life to this end:

Speak according to the people's power of comprehension and do everything that does not interfere with the attainment of the goal. In this way, you will bring men to lend a willing ear to the truth.

Take as much pleasure as necessary to preserve your health.

Try to acquire only as much money and other things as are needful to sustain life and health.

Observe the customs of the country insofar as they do not conflict with your aims.

We shall set forth Spinoza's philosophy according to the following schema:

The highest good is attained through the growth of philosophical insight in a vision of what is eternal (metaphysical total vision). Such insight is secured by a Theory of Knowledge. Both bring awareness of *what man is*.

The attainment of such insight is freedom and has as its consequence freedom in practical life (the ethical elucidation of servitude to the affects and of freedom through knowledge).

The personal freedom of the individual is not enough. We do not live singly, but in the real, social world, in which all depend upon all. Social existence is grounded in man and should be mastered by man. It is realized in the *state* and in the faith of *revealed religion*. While adhering to the recognized philosophical norms, Spinoza's thinking is always political and theological.

III. THE METAPHYSICAL VISION

If we are to understand Spinoza's manner of living and his judgment in ethical, scientific, political, and theological questions, we must consider the fundamental view that precedes everything else. It is to be sought in the metaphysical vision which dominated his life from the beginning to the end of his conscious development.

This total vision came to Spinoza suddenly, almost complete from the first moment. If it is asked how Spinoza arrived at it, only one answer is possible: By elucidation of his innate intuition of God. Awakened in him as a child by the Biblical tradition, this experience of God became for him the one thing on which everything else depended.

A. *Substance, attribute, mode*

These are the fundamental concepts with which Spinoza sets forth a vision of Being, illumined by his awareness of God. They may seem strange at first sight. To the question "What is?" he replies: Substance, its attributes and modes.

Substance: The source must be that which requires no further ground. When thought, it does not point beyond itself. In regard to it, the question "Whence?" falls silent. Substance is that which presupposes nothing other as its ground of being. In other words: substance is the ground which is ground, or cause, of itself *(causa sui).* Hence the concept of substance must not postulate the concept of another thing outside it. Substance is that which is in itself and is apprehended only through itself.

Concerning everything in the world, we can think that it might possibly not exist. But of the source, of substance and only of substance, we must say: It is conceivable only as existing. "By cause of itself I understand that whose essence involves existence, or that whose nature cannot be conceived unless existing." It would be a contradiction to conceive of substance as nonexisting. For this would be to think that nothing exists. Of course it is the easiest thing in the world to utter such a pseudo-thought, to say that it is possible that nothing exists. But really to think it out is impossible.

The being of Being—or of substance, as Spinoza calls it—is for him not a mere idea; it is the overwhelming, all-encompassing, infinitely rich intuition of God, which finds confirmation in all thought and experience, whenever we look into their ground.

Attribute: What we know of the one substance we know through its attributes, thought and extension *(cogitatio* and *extensio).* Everything we experience is either the one (from inside) or the other (from outside). They are called attributes, on the one hand "in respect to the understanding which imputes a certain nature to substance." On the other hand, attribute expresses *(exprimit)* or explains *(explicat)* the essence of substance. In their qualitative determination, the attributes are two (thought and extension), but each of these, like substance, is infinite and thinkable only through itself. But the attributes are infinite only in their kind, not absolutely infinite like substance. For substance has not only these two attributes, but infinitely many attributes that are unknown to us.

Mode: Modes are the individual things, *these* modes of thought and *these* bodies. They are "that which is in another thing through which also it is conceived." Substance and its attributes are eternal and infinite, the modes are temporal and finite. Since substance is God, Spinoza says: "Individual things are nothing but affections or modes of God's attributes, expressing those attributes in a certain and determinate manner."

What is can be stated in the one sentence: There is only substance and its attributes or the affections of the attributes. And: "All things, which are, are in God, and nothing can either be or be conceived without God."

B. *God*

To conceive of substance means to know God. Let us look more closely into Spinoza's idea of God.

1) *God exists.* Why is the thinking of substance or of God one with the knowledge that He exists?

That something exists is made certain by our existence. But our existence is transient; each individual existence is not necessary but contingent. We can think that it is not. Its Being must have a ground. We can find a ground of this existence in another, and of this second existence in still another, and so on *ad infinitum,* without ever arriving at an absolute ground. Such an absolute ground can lie only in a necessary existence, that is, an existence which does not exist contingently through something else, but through itself. But such an existence is necessary only if it is impossible to think that there is nothing. If nothing could be, Being would not be necessary.

Let us recapitulate: If we attempt to think that the mere finite beings we are and those we encounter in the world exist necessarily, it "follows that things finite are more powerful than the absolutely infinite Being." Only infinite, not finite, beings can exist necessarily. Hence the conclusion: "Either nothing exists, or Being absolutely infinite also necessarily exists."

Once again: It is inconceivable that only what is not necessary exists. But we finite, contingent beings exist. "And so of no existence can we be more sure than of the existence of the being absolutely infinite or perfect, that is to say, God."

This is for Spinoza the clearest, most definite, greatest of all certainties. Once substance is thought in earnest, doubt must vanish. "If anyone, therefore, were to say that he possessed a clear and distinct, that is to say, a true idea of substance, and that he nevertheless doubted whether such a substance exists, he would forsooth be in the same position as if he were to say that he had a true idea and nevertheless doubted whether or not it was false."

In this fundamental idea concerning the existence of God we must distinguish two elements: (1) it starts from the existence of finite things, but (2) the existence of the infinite substance as such is absolutely necessary. The derivation is only a thread guiding us from what is self-evident to our everyday consciousness (our existence) through the question of the ground of this existence (since there is nothing to be gained by an endless regress from object to object in the world) to the idea of necessary existence. For Spinoza the idea of substance or God is a certainty, not through derivation, but in itself. The idea of God requires no grounding or derivation. Rather, it precedes everything else. It is clear and certain in itself. Consequently, Spinoza rejects the proofs in which God's existence is inferred from the existence of the world. When theologians working with such proofs accused Spinoza of atheism, he attacked them on the strength of his original certainty of God's existence. He expressed surprise that they should call him an atheist; on the contrary, he said, those who needed such threadbare proofs were not certain of God's existence.

2) *God is infinite.* The substance that necessarily exists is infinite. If it were not, it would not exist through itself alone, but in relation to something

other. Nor would it be total being, that is, all reality. Substance or God is therefore absolutely infinite. It has infinitely many attributes: "The more reality of being a thing has, the more attributes it possesses expressing necessity or eternity and infinity. Nothing consequently is clearer than that Being absolutely infinite is necessarily defined as Being which consists of infinite attributes." Every attribute is also infinite, but only in its kind (*in suo genere*) and not absolutely.

We men know only two attributes: thought and extension. But if there were only these two attributes, substance would not be absolutely infinite. God's infinity allows of no limitation. In its knowledge of God, to be sure, the human mind can attain to no other attribute besides these two. It can neither disclose nor understand any other. The infinite number of attributes which man must necessarily conceive of bears witness to God's transcendence. The clearest knowledge of God must therefore stop at the overwhelming unknowableness of the godhead with its many attributes.

3) *God is indivisible.* In God, or substance, there is no division. There is no distinction between potentiality and actuality. What God was able to create, He also did create. In God's infinite intellect there is nothing that does not exist in reality.

In particular, freedom and necessity are one and inseparable in God. "In truth, God acts with the same necessity with which He understands Himself." In other words: "Just as it follows from the necessity of the divine nature that God understands Himself, with the same necessity it follows that God does infinite things in an infinite way."

God's freedom is not the arbitrary free will that men believe they possess, but action without outward compulsion, without dependence on deficiency and need, on purposes and a good that remains to be attained, but solely from out of His own essence. This freedom is identical with necessity.

Those who look upon God as a person see God's freedom in His arbitrariness and His power in His ability to do whatever He wills. Spinoza replies: Such power would actually be a limitation of His power, it would not be the infinity of His action, which is both free and necessary, but a determinate choice between possibilities, a lapse into the finite.

God's infinite action is indivisible and omnipresent. "Thus it is just as impossible for us to conceive of God not acting as of God not being."

4) *God is one.* If there were several different substances none would be substance, because it would be limited by something else. Thus in the nature of things there cannot be several substances, but only a single one. Nor can one substance be produced by another. "Hence it follows with the greatest clearness that God is one, that is to say, in nature there is but one substance, and it absolutely infinite."

But this unity and uniqueness of God is not that of the number one.

When we perceive an entity, we first, in view of its existence, speak of one or several exemplars. We "subsume things under a number only after we have brought them under a common genus." Hence, "we cannot call any thing one or single until we have conceived of another thing that accords with it." But since God's essence and existence are one and the same, it would be inappropriate to speak of Him as one. "Since we can form no general idea of His essence, he who calls God one or single has no true idea of God, or is speaking of Him inappropriately." "Only very improperly can God be called one or single."

Even in this first idea, which seemingly subjects God to determination, Spinoza transcends such determination by declaring that God's unity and singleness must not be conceived as the unity and singleness of things in the world. In formulation such contradiction is inevitable. Spinoza calls God one and withdraws his statement as inappropriate. And yet for finite man the statement that "God is one" remains in force.

5) *God is indeterminable and unimaginable.* It is Spinoza's philosophical purpose to purify his own consciousness of God's greatness and of God's reality as the only authentic existing power. Consequently he is tireless in combating false ideas of God. We can only think God. All reifications, determinations, imaginations cloud our consciousness of God. Spinoza criticizes all ideas of God which effect such determinations. They impinge on God's truth. They take a finite (worldly) reality for God's all-encompassing infinite reality. They set something else up as God in God's place.

This is what the populace does. They endow God with human faculties. "God is seen by the people as a man or in the image of a man." If triangles and circles had consciousness—says Spinoza, varying the old ideas of Xenophanes—they would conceive of God as triangular or circular. The notion of Jesus as a God-man is just such an error. "Certain churches maintain that God took on human nature. I have stated expressly that I do not know what they mean. In fact, quite frankly, what they say strikes me as just as absurd as if someone were to tell me that a circle had assumed the nature of a square."

They conceive of God's faculty of free will roughly as follows: God can do what He wills. He has a right to everything that is; He has the power to destroy everything and send it back to nothingness. They look upon God's power as the power of kings. In opposition to this, the purity of Spinoza's idea of God impels him to say: "No one will be able to understand properly what I have in mind unless he takes good care not to confuse God's power with human power or the right of kings."

The basic reason for such error is that God cannot be imagined but can only be thought. In thought nothing could be clearer and more certain. But every representation or imagination limits Him: "To your question whether I have as clear an idea of God as I have of a triangle, I answer in the affirmative. But if you ask me whether I have as clear a mental image of God as I have of a triangle, I shall answer No. For we cannot imagine God, but we can, indeed, conceive Him."

To imagine God as a person is in itself such a limitation. God has neither understanding nor will, but the attribute of thought, from which understanding and will issue as modes. He has neither motion nor rest, but the attribute of extension, from which spring the modes of motion and rest. Understanding and will, like motion and rest, are created nature; they are not God Himself, but consequences of God.

"Personality" is an imagination which diminishes God by assimilating Him to ourselves. Only finite beings have something else confronting them, and they confront each other in their self-consciousness. They determine themselves and they determine purposes which they make their own. But God in His infinity causes such beings to arise as consequences, while He Himself is above any such determinateness. God desires nothing, lacks nothing, sets Himself no purposes. "One may not say that God demands anything of anyone and just as little that something is displeasing or pleasing to Him. All these are human attributes that have no place with God."

Spinoza's Biblical consciousness, secured by reason, of the overpowering presence and reality of God in all things forbids him to denature God through representations contrary to His transcendent nature. In his serene awareness of God, he rejects the tangible embodiments of God in cults and revelations, which obscure our conception of Him, in favor of the absolute certainty to be gained by meditating on His eternally present reality.

But revelations and cults and churches with their representations of the divine are a part of man's life. The people are attached to them. Spinoza acknowledges that this is necessary, a consequence of our finite essence. And he does not say that these representations are devoid of truth. He combats only the intolerance and violence which result from them. We shall have more to say of this in connection with Spinoza's philosophy of politics.

6) *God is far and near.* In Spinoza's thinking God is utterly different from the world and at the same time infinitely close to it. The difference is expressed in such sentences as the following: "His essence would have to differ entirely from our intellect and will, and could resemble ours in nothing except name. There could be no further likeness than that between the celestial constellation of Dog and the animal which barks."

He expresses the nearness by saying that everything is a consequence of God, that accordingly God is in all things. God is not separate from the world; He is not a cause that passes into it (*causa transiens*), but a cause that remains in it (*causa immanens*).

Thus the radical difference between substance and modes is combined with the fundamental idea that all things are through God and in God, and that God is in them. But God in turn is so radically other that things cannot have anything in common with Him, because they are in every respect modes and not substance.

In the infinite extension of His being, God is the absolutely other, but in His consequences He is present to the world and to us. His remoteness is the substance that exists through itself; His nearness expresses itself in the fact that this substance, by virtue of the two attributes that are known to us, is the nature in which we are.

It is a mark of the radical difference between God and the world that of God's infinitely many attributes only two are accessible to us; it is a sign of His nearness that these two are wholly present to us as attributes and modes of the divine substance. The infinitely many attributes signify God's transcendence, the two known attributes His immanence. Our human thinking is grounded in the infinite mode of thought, which in turn has its ground in the attribute of God's substance. Our thinking is radically different from God's thought, but it is a mode and expression of God's thought.

Doctrines which assert God's immanence in the world are termed pantheistic. Is Spinoza a pantheist? Such formulas are inapplicable to great philosophy. Spinoza is a pantheist only insofar as for him the world is in God, but he does not believe that God's being in the world is the whole of His being. On the contrary, God's Being in the world is to God's authentic Being as the two attributes are to the infinitely many attributes.

Recapitulation: Spinoza's godhead. Spinoza's God has no history and brings about no supersensory history. History is only in the world of the modes, which as a whole is as eternal as substance, whose eternal consequence it is. In this world of modes things come and go, but the whole remains. God is eternal and unchanging as in the great Biblical visions.

Spinoza's God is without personality, because He is without determinations, without imaginable qualities. In His infinity, He is to clear thinking the greatest of certainties, the only cause which is everywhere effective. Even where God is not recognized, He is the greatest of certainties.

Spinoza's God is a logical entity which, however, is arrived at by means that transcend finite logic (for Spinoza's thinking starts from principles and definitions that are logically untenable).

But this ahistorical, impersonal, logical entity has immense power, for it is the foundation of everything that Spinoza thinks and does. If we ask: How can a man live with an idea of God which forbids all representation, which withdraws all categorial definitions in our statements about God, which knows no revelation and sets God so high over everything that we

call purpose, commandment, good and evil, that He seems to vanish
beyond everything we know?—the answer must be sought in Spinoza's
life and judgment and concrete insight.

Spinoza has been accused of atheism on the ground that his substance
is "incapable of all predicates worthy of God." In view of Spinoza's
all-encompassing idea of God, in whose presence the world disappears,
Hegel thought it more accurate to call this philosophy acosmism than
atheism. Spinoza's philosophy cannot be subsumed under either of these
terms. It breaks through all such definitions.

Consequently there is more truth in such poetic judgments as: "Spinoza
was a God-intoxicated man" (Novalis). "Perhaps it is here that God has
been seen closest at hand" (Renan). "The infinite was his beginning and
end" (Schleiermacher).

c. *The two attributes*

Metaphysical systems begin with a concept of being, and on this foundation
a construction arises—in Spinoza's case through his concepts of attribute
and mode. If this construction is taken as a knowledge of objects in the
world, it becomes a mere rational prolongation without metaphysical content. The arguments raised against it have no bearing on the content but
are directed against the construction, taken as knowledge of the world.
This is what happened in connection with the two attributes of thought
and extension.

The mathematician Ehrenfried Walter von Tschirnhaus asked Spinoza:
Why do we not know more than two attributes? Spinoza could not prove
it, he merely stated it to be so.

Tschirnhaus asked further: If there are infinitely many attributes of God,
there must be beings that know nothing of extension, to whom extension
would be as strange and unimaginable as to us the attributes of God perceived by them? Spinoza gives no answer.

Tschirnhaus asked finally: Are there totally unknown worlds (*modi*)
that spring from the infinitely many attributes that are unknown to us?
Spinoza referred him in answer to his scholion to Proposition 7 in the second part of the *Ethics*. We look it up. In this passage he writes that the
order and interrelation of ideas is the same as the order and interrelation
of things, because all attributes belong only to a single substance. "Whether
we think of nature under the attribute of extension, or under the attribute
of thought, or under any other attribute whatever, we shall discover one
and the same order." According to the aspect in which we see it, we must
explain the order of all nature solely by the attribute of thought or solely
by the attribute of extension, "and so with other attributes. Therefore God
is in truth the cause of things as they are in themselves, insofar as He con-

sists of infinite attributes, nor for the present can I explain the matter more clearly."

This is no answer to Tschirnhaus' question. One might continue to beset the silent Spinoza and ask: In view of the coincidence of orders, must not all attributes be present in all phenomena through the one substance? But since only two are present for us, are the others present in other worlds of modes? If this is not the case, why does only the world of the two attributes in which we ourselves are modes exist, and in what form are God's infinitely many attributes realized? But if there is a multiplicity of worlds which in their modes appear (express, explain themselves) on the basis of essentially different attributes, are there any indications of their existence? Are there for example worlds lacking the attribute of thought as our world lacks the infinitely many attributes apart from the two?

Spinoza neither asked these questions nor answered them when raised. Why not? Because the idea of the infinite attributes serves him only as an apt expression for God's transcendence; it does not lead him to spin fantasies of other worlds. The infinitely many attributes are for him an expression of a limit to our knowledge, not a field to be investigated. In general Spinoza's thinking is not directed toward the unknown and unknowable, but only toward actual reality. Hence God's being can at one and the same time be for him the totally other in the obscurity of the infinite and the totally lucid in the most certain knowledge.

How are the two attributes related? Is there a difference in rank between thought and extension? For Spinoza there is none. Spinoza argues against those who distinguish between "extensive substance" and divine substance, declaring the former to be unworthy of God, hence a mere creation of God, a created substance.

To be sure, Spinoza denies God's corporeality. "There are those who imagine God to be like a man, composed of body and soul." By body "we understand a certain quantity possessing length, breadth and depth, limited by some fixed form; to attribute these to God, a being absolutely infinite, is the greatest absurdity."

But it is something very different "to remove altogether from the divine nature substance itself corporeal or extended, affirming that it was created by God." That is a fallacy. For there can be no substance outside of God, nor can any be conceived of. Hence extended substance must be one of God's attributes.

In order to understand this correctly, we must bear in mind the meaning of "attribute" for Spinoza: in the attribute of extension substance remains infinite and indivisible. Only if we suppose extension to be finite and divisible, confusing it with the modes, do the contradictions arise which make it impossible for us to regard it as an attribute of God. Similarly it is false to argue that because corporeal substance is divisible, it is acted upon, but that

God cannot be acted upon. No, only the modes are acted upon, and not indivisible, infinite substance. While modes as affections of substance are finite, divisible, and particular, corporeal substance (in the attribute of extension, matter) can only be everywhere the same, infinite, indivisible, one. It would be absurd to conceive of it as manifold, composed of finite parts. Consequently, it is not unworthy of the divine nature. Thus it is false to say that by attributing extension to God Spinoza "naturalized" Him, if we take account of what the attribute of extension meant to Spinoza.

It might further be asked whether the supposed equality of all the attributes is not negated by a priority of thought. For all other attributes, it would seem, must be thought, whereas only thought thinks itself. Thus extension and all the other unknown attributes seem to confront thought as an attribute unique in its kind. This is another question that Spinoza does not ask. The only other attribute known to us is extension. In Spinoza it does not occupy a lower rank than thought.

All these arguments against Spinoza have the value of showing what Spinoza is not talking about. It must be admitted that Spinoza invited such criticism by his method of mathematical proof, which cannot help moving in the area of finite determination. If Spinoza has nothing to say in the face of such arguments, it is not, as one might think, because they are well founded, but only because the vision of God, which he is trying to explicate, makes him regard them as nonessential.

The essential is that by declaring extension to be an attribute of God, he has restored divinity and sanctity to the world. No aspect of reality is without God or opposed to God.

D. *The modes*

Individual things taken together (*omnia*) are the world. They are modes. Let us now examine in some detail the process in which the world is constituted, starting from substance and passing through the attributes of thought and extension, to the modes.

Individual beings are finite. The totality of these finite beings, each of which exists through another, is endless. Finite individual beings belong to the totality of the finite, which itself is endless and infinite. This infinity is a consequence of God's infinity, but is itself grounded in a third infinity, that of the infinite modes, which are not God's infinity and not the endlessness of individual things, but between the two. They are: the infinite intellect (*intellectus infinitus*), corresponding to the attribute of thought, motion and rest (*motus et quies*), corresponding to the attribute of extension, and the whole of the world (*facies totius universi*). The individual things (*res particulares*) are situated in the whole of the world.

Thus Spinoza conceives of a series extending from substance as *natura naturans* to *natura naturata* as the totality of the modes, and another series within it, from the infinite modes to the individual things. In the world of individual things the two attributes of substance are expressed as ideas and bodies. On the one hand, the series runs from thought (the attribute of *cogitatio*) to the infinite intellect (as an infinite mode) to ideas as finite modes of thought (*modi cogitandi*); on the other, from space (the attribute of extension) to motion and rest (as an infinite mode) to the finite modes of bodies. Both series run from substance through the whole of the world (infinite mode: *facies totius universi*) to the individual things, which, according to their aspect, we see as ideas or bodies.

The whole of the world or of nature is "one individual, whose parts, that is to say, all bodies, differ in infinite ways, without any change of the whole individual."

The totality of nature would be known if we knew how every part is related to the whole and to the other parts. But such knowledge "is beyond me, for it would require a knowledge of all nature and of all its parts." Thus all that can be obtained is the conviction "that each part of nature accords with the whole and with the other parts." But this conviction is grounded in metaphysical vision or in the idea of God.

From the two attributes of substance it follows: that in nature we apprehend only bodies and modes of thought (*modi cogitandi*), and that all things are extension *and* thought. Where there is thought there is extension, and where there is extension there is thought. Thought and extension do not act upon one another, but since both are rooted in the attributes of substance, "the order and connection of ideas is the same as the order and connection of things." The body and its idea, the idea and its body are one and the same thing, considered under one or the other attribute.

Here again we run into considerable difficulties if we try to consider this view of the world as an object of scientific knowledge. Are thought and body conceived in the relation of thought to its object or as a parallel between two independent series of events? There are suggestions of both possibilities in Spinoza. But although Spinoza clearly distinguished the infinity of scientific inquiry in the world from the fundamental metaphysical knowledge of the world's Being (in the first case, enduring fundamental ignorance, in the second total and ultimate conviction), his propositions are not without contradiction. In particular, it remains unclear to what extent the investigation of the relation between body and soul is possible in practice and in what sense the parallel between two independent but coinciding series is to be taken. Mistakenly, yet encouraged by statements of Spinoza, the proponents of the so-called theory of psychophysical parallelism in nineteenth-century psychology invoke his authority. In any event it is necessary, in studying Spinoza, to distinguish between those conceptions of the world which are elements in his vision of metaphysical being and those of his ideas which are subject to confirmation or refutation in scientific experience.

E. *Time; necessity*

The world is seen under aspects of spatial extension and thought. Time does not pertain to Being itself, to substance, but only to the modes. What is duration in time is eternity in the realm of Being. Thus under the concept of duration we can only explain the existence of the modes; we can conceive of substance only under the concept of eternity. We can conceive of the duration of the modes as longer and shorter, but substance admits of no such conceptions. "In eternity there is no *when* nor *before* nor *after*." To know things philosophically means to know them in their eternity. But when we "conceive of duration and magnitude abstractly, detached from substance and from the way in which they are descended from the eternal things, time and measurement arise; time by which to determine duration and measure by which to determine magnitude in the manner easiest for us to apprehend." But philosophical insight can penetrate and transcend all knowledge and all representations of finite things: "It is of the nature of reason to perceive things under a certain form of eternity."

While Spinoza sees everything in God and through God, and knows things in their eternity, he derives his perfect serenity from the idea of *necessity*.

With the category of "necessity" he goes beyond the definite necessities that we recognize in the world: the necessity of natural laws as rules governing the temporal process by which the individual, finite modes emerge from one another guides him to that other necessity, in which all things issue eternally from God, that is, from substance and its attributes.

The necessity of the causal relation among the modes is perceived by experience *ad infinitum* and can never be fully known. The necessity of the eternal emergence or being of all things is known intuitively. This intuitive knowledge can be secured and expressed by logical thought.

The natural laws of the endless modes may serve as a metaphor for the natural law of eternal necessity, but they are not the same thing. The former signify outward necessity or constraint, the latter inner necessity or freedom.

Spinoza delights in the experience of necessity. He expresses it over and over again with the serenity of his idea of God: The infinite follows in an infinite way from God. Everything that is is included in this necessity. For "all things, I say, are in God, and everything which takes place takes place by the laws alone of the infinite nature of God, and follows from the necessity of His essence." This necessity and these consequences are timeless; they follow "in the same way as it follows from the nature of a triangle from eternity to eternity, that its three angles are equal to two right angles." Hence *causa* and *ratio* are here the same (for where thought in categories goes beyond categories, the determinateness of the category ceases). The idea of this necessity leaves logical necessity, causality, providence, and destiny behind it, and can employ them all in turn as vanishing metaphors.

God's necessity is freedom, but not the limited freedom of the arbitrary. Hence it is an absurdity and a denial of freedom to say that God can cause it not to follow from the nature of a triangle that the sum of its angles is equal to two right angles.

Nietzsche took over this attitude toward necessity, this peace in necessity: "Shield of necessity! Supreme luminary of being—which no desire attains, which no negation sullies, eternal affirmation of being, I say yes to you eternally: for I love you, O eternity!"

F. *The cleavage between God and the world and the question of their unity*

The profoundest cleavage in the totality of Being is that between substance and its attributes on the one hand and the modes on the other hand, or, in traditional language, between God and the world. It is a cleavage between the infinite and the finite:

The infinite exists in itself, the finite always exists through some other finite thing: the former is *causa sui,* the latter caused by another finite thing; that is to say: the infinite contains existence in itself; the finite has its existence from another finite thing; the infinite is apprehended in itself, the finite through another. The infinite is unlimited, the finite limited by something else; the infinite is unconditioned, the finite conditioned. And everything that exists is either the one or the other, "is either in itself or in something other." Being-through-itself and being-through-something-other designates the absolute cleavage between God and things in the world.

Only the finite is individualized; the infinite is one. Hence where there is individuation, there is finiteness. "Every species of which more than one individual can exist must necessarily have an outward cause for its existence." Infinity and uniqueness go together, as do finiteness and indidividuation.

In its perfect positiveness the infinite excludes all determinations. The "determinations" of the infinite, the attributes, are themselves infinite and hence not determining predicates, but manifestations. Every determination is limitation, hence negation (*omnis determinatio est negatio*), and pertains to the finite. In the infinite there is no negation, but only positiveness. Any predicates that are imputed to it must be withdrawn forthwith (in the manner of negative theology).

This is the greatness of such thinking as Spinoza's: ordinarily we see the positive and concrete in definite finite figures. The Encompassing is in danger of becoming empty for us. Since we find nothing tangible in it, we suppose it to be nothing. Only what we can demonstrate, take hold of, differentiate has reality for us. Spinoza, to be sure, enters into this manifold just as we do, but coming from somewhere else, from God. For him God alone is wholly positive, and measured by God, every concrete thing is a mode, determined by negation. As a finite being, Spinoza too was obliged to live in the finite manifold, but as a rational being he was able, permeated through and through by the One, to see the negative irradiated by, and transcended in, the positive. Accordingly God and the world, one and all (*hen kai pan*), became the motto of those who shared Spinoza's faith.

Every single finite thing is caused by another finite thing *ad infinitum* ("transitive cause"). But the finite taken as a whole is caused by God ("immanent cause"). Thus if everything that exists exists in God, the question arises: Are God's infinite attributes different from the finite individual things? For these too are in God, or else they would not be. But their being-in-God is of a different nature, because the relation of finite individual things (the modes) to God is not only direct, but also indirect, by way of finite connections. Spinoza states this as follows: "The idea of an individual thing actually existing has God for a cause, not insofar as it is infinite, but insofar as it is considered to be affected by another idea of an individual thing actually existing, of which idea also He is the cause insofar as He is affected by a third, and so on *ad infinitum*."

The relation between substance and the modes or between God and the world is the ancient, never-to-be-solved question of the metaphysicians, who, however, each in his own way, seem to think they have solved it. Why, if the godhead is perfect, should there be a world at all? It is possible to draw up a schema of the possible solutions: Either a transition from God to world is conceived, or both are seen in such an opposition that the world vanishes and becomes mere illusion (but here the question remains: What is the source of the illusion?). Or God and world are conceived as one and the same. In the first case, the world is seen as creation (by God's will and decision) from matter or from nothing. Or as an overflowing from the One in a descending scale of Being. Or it is seen as an unfolding on an ascending scale. In the second case, the world is a phantasmagoria, an illusion, a dream, a mass hallucination, such as those provoked by magicians. It owes its existence solely to the radical delusion of men. It does not exist through God but through an error. In the third case the world is itself God. The question "Whence the world?" loses its relevance because the world discloses itself not only as divine, but in its totality as God itself. There is no transcendent godhead, and there is no world but God.

It would be a great mistake to assign any of the great metaphysicians to a definite place in such a schema. The answers given in the schema all have the definiteness that is possible and requisite in the knowledge of finite objects. But the later metaphysicians master the entire schema. They do not think in terms of finite objects, their thought is a transcending. Hence their positions have always been assailed from the standpoint of logical analysis, which deals in defined concepts, because, seen from outside, they reveal contradictions. Such is also the case with Spinoza.

He seems to reject all the positions noted in the above schema: creation, for God has neither intellect nor will; the descending overflow, for the connection is eternal, while time exists only in the series of the modes; upward development, for Being is eternal presence, there has been no progress. And Spinoza would also have to reject the notion that the world is illusion. For he explains it not only on the basis of human representation, but as the eternal necessity of a mode of existence which does indeed exist. Spinoza expressly rejects the unity of God and world as one substance, whose parts are individual things. God is not world matter, from whose division the things come into being; He is indivisible substance, while the individual things are not substance but modes, divisible, coming into being and passing away.

But what does Spinoza think? In vain we look for a precise formulation of the question and an unequivocal answer. He speaks in metaphors which indicate that all existing things must be understood as a consequence of the one substance. There are not two modes of being, God and world, hence he cannot inquire into the relation between them; there is only the one being, which expresses itself, explicates itself, has necessary consequences. According to Spinoza, everything follows as necessarily in eternity as it follows from the concept of the triangle that the sum of its angles is equal to two right angles. Yet this too is a metaphor; the two consequences are not the same: the metaphysical consequence is "as" the mathematical consequence.

An explanatory derivation of the world from its source in God is impossible, nor does Spinoza achieve any such thing. His thinking has its source in his original awareness of God, and the content of his expressed thought is a guide to that source.

Thus it is impossible to start from a source, however concretely conceived, in order to encompass all things in one. But it is still possible to think toward a source.

Where philosophy has misunderstood itself and derived the world from its ground, the metaphysical idea has degenerated into a hypothesis for the explanation of phenomena. Such a hypothesis has methodological justification only where the possibility of refuting or confirming it opens up the way to endless progress in the knowledge of the world. Metaphysics as a hypothesis of the world as a whole is meaningless. In metaphysical thinking derivation has another purpose: to express the mystery itself. It is a discourse addressed to the mystery, purporting to illuminate it, not to explain it.

But are we justified in interpreting Spinoza's ideas in this way? He stresses the cogency of his thinking, which excludes all contradictions and asserts itself by refuting contradictions. To stress the contradictions in his

thinking and interpret them meaningfully seems to run counter to his innermost intention. This objection can be answered by an exposition of Spinoza's theory of knowledge, which alone can give us an adequate logical insight into his metaphysical vision, which is, to be sure, arrived at and expressed by thinking, but cannot be fully encompassed by rational means. We shall speak of this in the next section.

Spinoza's schema of Being is extremely simple: substance, attributes, modes—and his thinking in these modes is uncommonly sober, even when God is substituted for substance and world for the modes. But the simplicity is deceptive: his edifice is complex and full of logical and epistemological difficulties. And the sobriety too is deceptive: this thinking is not cool, but burning; it embraces Spinoza's whole life, which it transforms into a pure flame in God's all-pervading presence.

Substance, attribute, mode are words drawn from ancient philosophical tradition. Their meanings have undergone many changes. "Substance" is the Latin translation of the Greek *hypokeimenon* (the underlying). But "substance" was also used as a translation for the Greek *ousia* (essence), more often translated directly as *essentia*. To these were added numbers of other words that were used in the same sense or for purposes of distinction. Eckhart translated substances as *"Selbstende Wesen"* (beings that produce a "self"). Leibniz translated substance as *Selbststand* (self-sufficiency). In following these sources of philosophical usage, we observe historical shifts of meaning, not in a single line, but in a complex interchange. By going back to the etymological origins, we arrive at a concrete meaning (as in the case of substance, as that which underlies the phenomenon) or at a symbol. All this is interesting, but what counts in philosophy is the imprinting of word meanings through great, new, original ideas, and the reinforcement of such meanings not through definition, which is always inadequate, but by the use of words in movements of thought. By taking advantage of the possible connotations of words, language becomes a medium for the communication of new ideas. Sometimes a word takes on a new richness of meaning that had never before been associated with it: examples of this are "the Idea" in Plato, "reason" in Kant, "existence" (Existenz) in Kierkegaard, and "substance" in Spinoza. Spinoza's "substance" is neither matter, nor the underlying, nor the enduring, nor any of the other things the word had previously meant, but a new and original word for the philosophical idea of God. *Attribute* means "what is attributed to," or "property." In this sense, "divine attributes" were a familiar concept. Spinoza took over the word and filled it with new content. *Mode* means manner, whether of being, or happening, or consciousness, or of figures of thought; it can also mean state. For Spinoza "mode" is the concept designating the common essence of all finite things.

It is to be noted that when philosophical concepts pass into general usage they lose their speculative connotation and resume their old tangible, concrete, finite meanings; thus "substance" becomes matter and "essence" a sublimated body; "mode" becomes species or the way in which something is done, while "attribute" becomes a distinctive property of things, etc. For an understanding of philosophical ideas, it is important that these familiar meanings should be clearly known; but they must be kept distinct from the speculative ideas to which, however, they may serve as guides.

IV. THEORY OF KNOWLEDGE

How does Spinoza know what he tells us? He answers this question by elucidating the ways in which we know. It is his theory of the stages of knowledge which first explains the nature of Spinoza's certainty that God, as the one and only reality, is present in our thinking.

A. *The stages of knowledge*

The three stages are set forth in the early treatise, *On the Improvement of the Understanding. First,* the delusion of opinion and imagination, fed only by hearsay or isolated experience. *Second,* true belief. *Third,* clear and distinct knowledge. The meaning of the stages is illustrated in an example. Given the problem, $2:3 = 4:x$, following the dictate of authority, I find the value of x by multiplying the second and third figures and dividing by the first, and verify by repetition and observation (first stage); or by drawing the correct inference from the rule of proportion (second stage); or else I "see" the fourth term on the strength of my intuition of proportion (third stage). In the first case, the arithmetical principle is not a truth for me but a mere opinion; in the second case, the truth is derived, in the third it is intuited. "But we term clear insight only that insight which is gained not by rational conviction, but by feeling and intuition of things themselves: this is far superior to the others."

In the later works, the three stages are further characterized. *First* stage: We perceive individual things in a mutilated, confused way through the senses—here we have "knowledge deriving from uncertain experience." Or signs and words remind us of such things and we imagine them with equal imprecision. This is the stage of opinion and imagination. *Second* stage: We have clear and distinct common concepts (*notiones communes*); these are adequate ideas of things. We operate with them in the second kind of knowledge, *reason* (*ratio*). *Third stage:* Intuitive knowledge (*scientia intuitiva*) attains "to an adequate knowledge of the essence of things."

In this theory of knowledge, two distinctions are essential: between imagination (*imaginatio*) and intellect (*intellectus*), and between reason and intellect.

1. "There are many things to which we can never attain by imagination but only with the intellect." Substance, eternity, and metaphysical concepts in general are not imaginable objects. We come up against confusing concepts and insoluble problems "if we have not distinguished between what we only understand but cannot imagine and what we can also imagine."

Spinoza illustrates his meaning by the example of magnitude. It can be conceived in two ways: abstractly and superficially, as we imagine it (then it is finite, divisible, has measure), or in its eternal essence, as it is known by the intellect alone. In the imagination, the infinite is held to be greater or smaller than another infinite, and itself divisible; the intellect conceives of it as indivisible and incommensurable with anything else.

"If anyone attempts to explain such things with concepts that are mere expedients of the imagination, he is doing nothing more than were he to strive to lose his mind by means of his imagination." The mind is confused by the expedients of the imagination. We move away from being by transforming it into imagination. In the imagination that which is beyond all thingness is transformed into a thing. An example: time is generally thought to be composed of moments; but this is no better than to mistake number for a mere aggregate of zeroes. All those concepts "by which the common people are in the habit of explaining nature are only different sorts of imaginations, and do not reveal the nature of anything in itself, but only the constitution of imagination."

2. In the realm of thought (which is always held apart from the imagination) Spinoza takes over a traditional distinction but gives it a special form: on the one hand, *intellectus* (intellect), on the other, *ratio* (reason). The reason of the second stage obtains knowledge indirectly, through inferences. The intellect of the third stage has immediate knowledge. Only when we see a thing is it present to us; only then are we, in a manner of speaking, one with it. Thus reason with its inferences and derivations merely points the way; the goal is attained only in immediate intuition.

In common usage, intellect and reason are synonymous. A distinction between them is essential for the philosopher, because the two refer to fundamentally different certainties; the one attained indirectly, discursively, by logical inference; the other immediate, intuitive, attained by a logical vision. This intuition is not sensory intuition in space and time, and it is not psychic, emotional experience; it is an asensory, luminous intuition in timeless presence.

It is generally supposed that we need sense perception, not only in order to have a real object (which is correct), but also in order to experience reality as such, and that thought becomes empty when it is not supported or filled by sensory intuitions. What philosophers have said concerning another, supersensory intuition is regarded as fantasy, mystical fiction, absurdity.

Within the limits of our human existence, knowledge of the third variety can be communicated and acquire self-certainty only in the forms of reason (the second variety). Hence rationality is the eternal medium for what is more than rationality (namely, the intuitive thinking of the intellect). Without this "more," mere rationality is endless and empty. Rationality, meditation in rational movements, takes on content only if the presence of God is expressed in it. Though free from sensory experience, reason is not self-sufficient; only through its experience of the intellect as a timeless, ever present source does reason become the language of truth, which expresses eternal reality.

Spinoza was determined not to confuse the sources of our knowledge. In the *empirical world* we have experience *ad infinitum,* nothing is ever complete, everything is relative. Our experience of *reality* is always present; we are and remain in a self-sufficient realm of absolute perfection. When this experience enters into time, it is explicated in movements of thought, whose purpose it is to return whence they came.

This supreme knowledge is the knowledge of God; it is "not a consequence of something else, but immediate." For "God is the cause of all knowledge, which is known solely through itself and not through something else." And "we are by nature so united with Him that without Him we cannot subsist and cannot be conceived of."

The source of the insight which is at the center of Spinoza's thinking is God's presence. This is stated very clearly even in his early writings. In the earliest treatise, written in Dutch, the *Short Treatise on God, on Man, and His Well-Being,* the distinction is made between *verstand* (*intellectus*) and *reeden* (*logos, ratio*). And here Spinoza also states clearly the decisive practical consequence of this distinction: the proper use of intellect and reason liberates us from the affections that enslave us. "I say: our intellect, because I do not believe that reason alone has the power to liberate us from all these," since reason has no power to lead us to the attainment of our well-being, which results "from a direct revelation of the object itself to our intellect. And if that object is glorious and good, then the soul becomes necessarily united with it."

Here Spinoza presents an analogy to certain historical doctrines: to the "inner light," to the "spirit" through which the believer understands the Bible, to the highest rung of contemplation in the thinking of the mystics— but also to Kant's Ideas and reflecting judgment, through which all the investigations of the understanding first acquire meaning and systematic significance.

The distinction between the second and third varieties of knowledge is crucial for Spinoza's thinking. But since the second is in the service of the third and provides the field in which what is "seen" in the third is communicated, Spinoza sometimes speaks of them in one breath, or seems to use them interchangeably. (If we translate Spinoza's *intellectus* as "understanding—as he himself does in his Dutch letters—and his *ratio* as "reason," his use of the terms becomes the opposite of Kant's. Insofar as a comparison is possible, Kant's "understanding" is Spinoza's "reason," and conversely.)

B. *Ideas*

By idea Spinoza means "a conception of the mind which the mind forms because it is a thinking thing." But Ideas also have objective existence (there are Ideas in God): they "are the same and will continue to be so, even if neither I nor any man has never thought of them." The Ideas in themselves are adequate or inadequate; they are from the start a unity of idea and will, active insofar as they are adequate, passive insofar as they are inadequate; adequate Ideas possess perfect certainty, capable of withstanding all doubt.

Adequate and inadequate ideas: By an adequate idea Spinoza means "an idea insofar as it is considered in itself, without reference to the object." As such, it "has all properties of a true Idea." These are "internal signs," whereas that which is external, the agreement, namely, of the idea with its object, "must be excluded." But a consequence of the truth is that "A true idea must agree with its object."

By inadequate ideas Spinoza means mutilated (incomplete) and confused ideas. Among its modes of thought, our mind encompasses love, desires, and all the affections, which, however, are dependent for their existence on our idea of a loved or desired thing. A pure idea, on the other hand, can exist without the presence of any other mode of thought. There are ideas without affections. When in the common order of nature the human mind perceives and is acted upon by the outside objects with which it accidentally comes into contact, or when it knows itself amid the affections of the body, its ideas are confused and inadequate. Only when the mind is moved from within, as when it considers several objects at once, and understands their similarities and the differences and oppositions between them, can it have adequate ideas.

The nature of this pure thinking of the ideas is clarified by Spinoza's distinction between common notions and universal notions. Universal notions are generic concepts such as horse, man, dog. Since they designate only what is universal in things, they are incomplete concepts, accompanied by different representations in each man who thinks them. Other universal concepts are essence, thing, something. They arise because the limited human body can form only a limited number of clear images at once.

Where the limit is passed, the images become confused and are collected, as it were, under a concept such as essence, thing, something. "These terms signify ideas in the highest sense confused."

The common concepts on the other hand are those that are common to all men; they are complete and form the basis of pure thought. In contrast to the mutilating abstraction of the universal, they designate the common essence of things. Such common concepts are extension and thought and in the highest degree God. "The human mind has adequate knowledge of God's eternal and infinite essence."

Idea and will: In Spinoza idea and will are one and the same. Will is more than desire, it is the power to affirm or negate. But affirmation and negation are bound up with ideas. "In the mind there is no volition or affirmation and negation excepting that which the idea, insofar as it is an idea, involves." An idea is not a static image, "a mute painting," but acts by affirmation and negation. An adequate idea is not passive but expresses an action of the mind.

The usual distinction between intellect and will (and the resulting opposition between intellectualism and voluntarism) is not relevant to Spinoza. Pure volition resides in pure thought, and conversely. An idea that is not effective is not an idea; a will that is not illumined by the purest idea is no will. Only confused, passive thoughts and impulses are left when the One, which is at once idea and will, is veiled.

Hence necessity is an attribute both of the will and of the idea, and this in the highest degree in connection with God, who is free from all obscurity. Hence "God acts and understands Himself with the same necessity." God never acts arbitrarily like a despot, who has it in his power to destroy everything and restore it to nothingness; He has the freedom of necessity.

Spinoza attacks Bacon and Descartes for asserting that the will is free and superior to reason. Acts of the will, he says, do not have "the will" as their cause. Each particular act of will must have a cause of its own. The will is not, as Descartes supposed, the cause of error. An inadequate idea is untruth; it wills only passively.

Certainty: A true idea comprises certainty. Anyone who has a true idea knows it to be true. Anyone who has an adequate idea knows it. In other words: "Anyone who truly understands a thing has at the same time an adequate idea of his understanding." An idea is not a mute image, it is the very act of understanding. "Who can know that he understands a thing unless he first of all understands it?" This knowing-in-advance is the true idea. Nothing could be clearer or more certain than this idea, which is the norm of truth. "Just as light reveals both itself and the darkness, so truth is the standard of itself and the false." Truth illuminates itself and error as well, just as waking consciousness throws light on a dream.

A false idea on the other hand comprises no certainty but at most an

absence of doubt. "However much a man may cling to a falsehood, we shall
never say that he is certain of it. For by certainty we mean something positive
and not absence of doubt.

The ideas, the modes of thought which Spinoza looks upon as independent structures, as parts of the infinite divine intellect (the *modus infinitus*),
must not be identified with what we commonly call concepts or representations. An idea "is not an image of anything, nor does it consist of words.
For the essence of words and images is formed of bodily motions alone, which
involve in no way whatever the conception of thought."

c. *Relation to God*

In our knowledge we are guided either by experience or by the pure thinking
of adequate ideas. In our knowledge of the particular modes, experience is
the norm. Since individual modes are known through other individual
modes, this knowledge is never concluded. The knowledge of pure reason,
on the other hand, depends on thought alone. Without experience of the
world, this knowledge attains to Being itself. The necessity of thinking
implies the existence of what is thought. In other words: that which must
necessarily be thought also exists. Or: thinking and Being are identical. But
this is true only of substance, of God's eternal Being, and of what eternally
follows from it. Hence particular things as such do not disclose the necessity of thought. However, the existence of the modes as a whole is conceived
as necessary, and similarly, each individual thing, insofar as it is seen "under
a certain mode of eternity" (*sub quadam specie aeternitatis*). Experience
knows things to be real "in relation to a particular time and place." But
when the mind conceives these things from the standpoint of eternity, it
knows them to be necessary.

Particular things do not exist without God and cannot be conceived of
without God. However, God does not belong to their essence. Hence the
twofold aspect of particular things: on the one hand they can be investigated
endlessly, but on the other hand we can have complete and fundamental
knowledge of their mode of being.

Since everything is in God and known in God, it becomes necessary "to
observe the right order in philosophizing." Spinoza, who from the outset
orients his entire inquiry toward the knowledge of God, denies that individual things can be properly known without the knowledge of God. God
is the first, the fundamental. The sciences of things in the world become
aimless and meaningless if only their never concluded findings are considered. They are all ways to the knowledge of God, and take on meaning as
such. Accordingly, Spinoza attacks those who have reversed the order of
knowledge: "For although the divine nature ought to be studied first, because it is first in the order of knowledge and in the order of things, they

think it last; while, on the other hand, those things which are called objects of the senses are believed to stand before everything else. Hence it has come to pass that there was nothing of which men thought less than the divine nature while they have been studying natural objects, and when they afterwards applied themselves to think about God, there was nothing of which they could think less than those prior fictions upon which they had built their knowledge of natural things, for these fictions could in no way help to the knowledge of the divine nature. It is no wonder, therefore, if we find them continually contradicting themselves."

D. *Spinoza's geometrical method*

Spinoza expounded his philosophy in his *Ethica Ordine Geometrico Demonstrata*. On the model of Euclid, he starts out with definitions and axioms; then come theorems and their proofs, and finally notes (*scholia*). In addition there are introductions and appendices.

Spinoza was convinced that his ideas were of rationally compelling certainty. He spoke of "philosophical or mathematical certainty." And in rejecting the false conception of God, he wrote: The human race would have been kept "in darkness to all eternity, if mathematics, which does not deal with ends, but with the essences and properties of forms, had not placed before us another rule of truth." But Spinoza's use of the mathematical form of exposition has been almost universally criticized as an error. The following objections to it can be made:

It is obvious that Spinoza's whole philosophy is contained in the unproved definitions and axioms for which he lays claim to immediate evidence. Thus the geometrical exposition is a great circle which recapitulates, and fills with concrete content, what must be granted from the first. But the fundamental concepts themselves lack the unequivocal clarity of geometrical definitions and axioms (and are far from being constructed according to the rules governing a modern system of mathematical axioms). Quite on the contrary, they are ambiguous, or unthinkable in rational terms, or plethoric—as metaphysical concepts have always been. Spinoza's basic concepts with their speculative character—which means precisely that they are rationally unthinkable—are not concepts of the kind that serve for unequivocally compelling operations, but inherent paradoxes by which to attain metaphysical certainty.

Spinoza's proofs leave us indifferent if we interpret them as compelling rational proofs, and moreover, if this is done, they prove not to be compelling at all. The proofs have force as a form of actualization. Spinoza carries out his proofs in the second category of knowledge (which in disregard of his own distinction he calls intellect *or* reason), that is, they are not based on perception and imagination or on the intuitive knowledge of the third category. But the proofs have meaning only when this last is present as a guide. The demonstrations as such are concerned with objects, oppositions, contradictions. But in this medium, there is a recollection or anticipation of intuitive knowledge, the world-transcending knowledge of God, and an appeal to the motives underlying a right conduct of life. It does not suffice to carry out the simple rational operations with the concepts as defined. We understand only if we are moved by the contents which these operations serve to elucidate.

One may judge this method to be unsuitable for philosophy. Descartes expressly rejected it. He points out that in mathematics simple, self-evident principles are the point of departure, while in philosophy they are the aim and goal (only once did Descartes employ the mathematical method of exposition, and then playfully). And it must indeed be admitted that Spinoza's method is inappropriate where others have tried to imitate it (cf. Schelling in his early works).

If nevertheless this unique work makes a profound impression, it is because Spinoza's use of mathematics as a metaphor for the knowledge of things eternal (of the rational power of cogent demonstration as a metaphor for the intuition of the third variety of knowledge) became an effective form of meditation. Spinoza does not seek certainty of God, he has it. He does not search for what is eternal, for the fixed and enduring relationships, but describes them. Thus it is in keeping with the nature of this philosophy that it should be set forth as an unfolding of the fundamental knowledge, in which whatever is implied in the fundamental concepts apprehended by intuition is made explicit. The aim is not to discover, but to clarify, not to advance, but to delve deeper by repetition. The demonstrations are a meditative elucidation of the unfathomable axioms.

Most readers are repelled by the demonstrations. This is unfortunate, for to think them through is to penetrate the inner structure of this conceptual edifice, which arrives at no conclusion but elucidates Spinoza's vision of Being and of life. Still, it must be admitted that the constant references to previous theorems make continuous reading very difficult. (By dropping the geometrical form and inserting the theorems to which Spinoza refers, Carl Gebhardt in his translation has obtained a readable text. But he has omitted many of the demonstrations, and moreover the work loses much of its expressive power when shorn of its geometrical form.)

Spinoza clearly understood the nature of his thinking, as he shows by his differentiation of the three classes of knowledge. But, although he always seems to be slipping back into the rationality of compelling logic, his fundamental idea is always at work: the essence of man is knowledge; in knowledge God Himself is present; the purest form of knowledge is mathematics, with its absolute clarity.

But though he speaks of "philosophical or mathematical method," Spinoza did not identify philosophy and mathematics. He chose an imitation of mathematical form as the most suitable way to communicate his vision. He chose mathematics as a metaphor, because he claimed unique and universal truth for his philosophical knowledge. The timelessness of logical and mathematical relations was for him the best possible symbol for the timeless truth and reality which disclose themselves only *sub specie aeternitatis*. The mathematical method thus becomes a metaphor for the fundamental metaphysical experience, in which things are seen "from the standpoint of eternity." In rationality the thinker gains certainty of what rationality as such can never attain.

E. *Mysticism, rationalism, speculative thought*

In view of Spinoza's description of the stages of knowledge, and its highest, the intellect, which in thought (*ratio*) ascertains and experiences eternal reality, the question arises: Do all these things exist? Are they not fictions? Are the examples of immediate mathematical intuition not irrelevant? But the heart of the matter is elsewhere. The essential is a manner of thinking, in which nothing is apprehended objectively but perfect certainty is obtained in union with the object, not through feeling but through thought.

Is it not overbold to affirm the unique self-certainty of our thinking in this process of transcending all rationality by rational means? Some incline to do so but lose courage. For everything is falsified where such certainty is denatured into a knowledge of something that we have and can state as we have and state our knowledge of objects in the world, of things that can be perceived by the senses, and of concepts that can be logically defined. When this is done, what in Spinoza was existential actuality in thinking loses all validity.

The Neo-Kantians have attacked Spinozism as uncritical dogmatism. Kant himself had no relation to Spinoza and scarcely studied him. Kant's criticism applies only to Spinozist perversions in which the philosophical core of Spinoza's thinking had been lost.

There is no doubt that Spinoza, who was far removed from critical thinking in the manner of Kant, gave ground for misunderstanding in his formulations. But this does not touch the heart of his philosophy. We may close our minds to such thinking. But then we must abandon the hope of understanding Spinoza (and all original metaphysicians). And for those who reject such thinking the question remains: What will they live by? For by sensory experience and rationality they cannot attain to any meaning that will sustain life; to live by sheer vitality like the animals is to renounce the possibilities of human existence. Or they may find the meaning in revelation—without, against, or above reason. On the plane where Spinoza moves, revealed faith is the only alternative, and it was indeed his only problem (we shall speak of it later).

Neither mysticism nor rationalism: Spinoza's philosophy has been called mystical, unjustly, if by mysticism is meant either the experience of union with the godhead (in which subject and object disappear) or of concrete supersensory visions. Spinoza knows no such experiences and denies them any character of truth. His pure thought, in which union with the godhead is achieved in the third stage of knowledge, merely presents an analogy to mysticism.

Spinoza has been called a rationalist. Nowhere has thought raised so vast a claim, nowhere has philosophical thought attained such heights of happiness. "Blissful through reason," said Nietzsche. In Spinoza, however, we find the "beatitude" not of the rationalist, who takes pleasure in explaining everything reasonably and in debunking everything he lays eyes on, but of the thinker who, indefatigably ascending and descending the ladder of stages, illumines the world and himself, who here in the world seeks means of communicating his insight; his is the beatitude which finds its fulfillment and justification in *amor intellectualis.* To call Spinoza a rationalist is to forget that his philosophy, conceived intuitively in the third category of knowledge and expressing itself through the second (*ratio*), is neither exhausted nor ultimately grounded in these kinds of knowledge.

Certain of Spinoza's positions remind us of Descartes and Malebranche (Descartes: *cogitatio* and *extensio;* Malebranche: the knowledge of all things in God). But their thinking moved against a background of ecclesiastical faith; they supported its authority without restriction. Their thinking could not achieve the philosophical earnestness of Spinoza, for it did not embrace man's most central concerns. In Pascal, on the other hand, authoritarian faith was carried to its most unexpected consequences, which most others have veiled, and so thought was devaluated. Spinoza differs from all these. For him thought is the summit of human power, God is in thought, and nothing is left in the background. Such thinking was bound to be different in every phase from that of the thinkers who set their faith in authority. Spinoza had the perfect earnestness which made possible complete peace and a purity of personal existence that cannot spring from a philosophy which already possesses a faith somewhere else, so that, robbed of its philosophical core, it degenerates into a factual discussion, questionable from the standpoint of science and irrelevant to faith.

What Spinoza does in his thinking: Our usual thinking is immersed in darkness. It moves in abstractions, schemata, types, and words which distort even our perception. Governed by conventions and prejudices, its vision and concept are blind.

All great philosophy strives for deliverance from the veils of distortion and forgetfulness, from the endless thinking which is meaningless for lack of aim or fulfillment, which loses itself because at every step its direction changes, and despairs when it takes stock of itself. But it is not enough to learn how to disregard prejudices and conventions and to "look at the things themselves": such an orientation is negative and destructive, the things seen become all equally indifferent. The essential and positive step is toward a fulfilled thinking, a thinking grounded in the substance of Being. Such is Spinoza's philosophizing. He carries out its operations and speaks of it with a grandiose simplicity and assurance. For without self-conscious action no speculative truth is possible.

The reader of Spinoza often starts out with the impression that he understands nothing, or that he is reading sheer nonsense. Such an attitude is only natural as long as we are immersed in the darkness of everyday life. Some stubbornly cling to it. Others leap into a mystical reverie, lose their footing in the world and cannot regain it; their spirit dwells worldless in the elsewhere, while they, in the flesh, carry on a random existence in the world. Spinoza is not one of these. His thinking leads beyond but does not lose the world. As in Kant the Idea does not exist without the understanding it governs, so Spinoza's thinking does not take leave of the living man it guides, even though the guidance is acquired in a ground that is fully disclosed only in pure thought. For "we do not need experience for that whose existence is not differentiated from its essence. Indeed, no experience can ever teach us anything about it."

But as finite modes, we are beings of mind and body, living in nature, hence bound to place and time, which we transcend in pure insight but do not for one moment leave.

On transcending with categories: The godhead is said to be without determinations, to be pure cause and necessity, without purposes. But each one of these statements effects a determination. Inevitably, when I think, I determine in categories. If with Spinoza I think necessity, ground, cause, effect, I am thinking just as much in categories as when I think in the categories of purpose and volition, which Spinoza rejects.

There are several methods of thinking beyond the categories in categories:

1. When Spinoza thinks necessity, he *compares.* He compares a necessity conceived as indeterminate and all-embracing with the determinate mathematical necessity in which one theorem follows timelessly from another. But eternal necessity is only *as* mathematical necessity, not identical with it. Again he compares eternal necessity to the necessity of the temporal principle of causality, but eternal necessity as an all-embracing power is only *as* the principle of causality, not identical with it. To think the absolute in definite categories is to effect differentiations that can give only a distorted view of it, such as we obtain in our representations. Thus categorial determination can be taken only as a comparison.

2. In another method different or opposite categories are identified. Spinoza says *causa sive ratio, intelligere sive agere, deus sive natura,* and so

on. Here cause and logical ground, thought and action, God and nature, are conceived as identical. It is easy to point out the "fallacy" in such identifications. Descartes made abundant use of this *sive* as a means of doing away with scholastic distinctions (e.g. *notiones sive idea, intellectus sive ratio, est sive existit*); here the identification is merely a leveling, which prepares the way for new concepts, and the loss of essential insights must be regarded as a negative element in Descartes. In Spinoza such identifications are powerful instruments of transcending thought (except in cases where inattention leads him to equate concepts—such as *ratio* and *intellectus*—between which he himself has drawn an essential distinction).

This method of positing differentiated and opposed categories as identical runs as follows: As differentiated and opposed, they can be determined; in the identification they become rationally unthinkable; their meaning becomes indeterminate, but thanks to their differentiated origins they do not become empty. Thus they become signs for the determination of the indeterminable. The statements are untrue (because contradictory) as assertions of fact, true as a transcending beyond determinations.

Spinoza used the method of categorial transcending, but he did not raise it to clear consciousness. It would be absurd to accuse him of failing to distinguish between *causa* and *ratio* and of coming to false conclusions by confusing them. He saw the difference very clearly. To have identified them despite this clarity was creative philosophical naïveté. In him it is possible, because his thought does not transcend but is fundamentally rooted in transcendence. He does not think toward God, but comes from God in his thinking of things. He knows that every determination makes for finiteness (*omnis determinatio est negatio*) and knows that thought operates in determinations. But all determinations are a guiding thread which enables us, by negating them, to arrive at the place where the thought that expresses itself in discourse (the thought which applies to the modes) is transcended in the authentic thought of that which is without determination.

But why did Spinoza prefer the categories of substance, necessity, ground, and eternity, and reject those of purpose and volition? A transcending in categories should after all be possible in all categories. This too we can only interpret as grandiose naïveté on the part of Spinoza, who in the one group of categories finds his consciousness of Being and his view of life confirmed, and in the other impaired. Quite apart from their function in his method of transcending, the categories become realities for him instead of remaining symbols of thought. In this he resembled all original metaphysicians. If with a method in view we undertake to transcend in categories and actually find this possibility in all the categories, we take the method as our starting point and our thinking becomes an unreal game, or else we are merely building up a thinking machine that we can call on whenever we need it. In true transcending, the reality of transcendence is present before the method, and speaks in the method. Then thinking ceases to be a game and becomes a means of elucidating reality itself in a real situation. What makes Spinoza so impressive is not that he invents methods, but that the reality of God is present in his thinking.

V. MAN

On the basis of what follows necessarily from God, of the infinite which follows from the infinite in infinite ways, Spinoza now sets out to explain that "which may lead us as it were by the hand to a knowledge of the human mind and its highest happiness." What man is, his consciousness of himself if he is authentic, that is, if he thinks in God, must guide his action and his life.

A. *Man is not substance but mode*

Substance, or God, is the essence which necessarily includes existence. Man's essence does not necessarily comprise existence. Rather, in the order of nature, it can "just as well come about that this or that man exists as that he does not exist." Hence, "the Being of substance does not pertain to the essence of man."

That men are not substances is further demonstrated by the fact "that they are not created but only engendered, and that their bodies existed previously, though shaped in another way."

Spinoza's intention is to show that man is infinitely remote from God and at the same time infinitely close to Him. No created things can exist and be thought without God, but God's nature does not belong to their essence. This is true also of man. Substance, or God, is infinitely more existent or more powerful than all the modes and hence also than man. But both are true: God is utterly other, infinitely remote with His infinitely many attributes, and God is present in us, though only with two attributes.

This tension between the remoteness and presence of God, which in Spinoza's thinking is at the same time peace—the peace of being in God, though infinitely far away from Him—disappears when, arguing objectively, we try to pin him down to one or the other position. (1) We take Spinoza at his word and try to force him to be consistent: in man, to be sure, there are only two attributes, but through these alone he is a part of God. But in this case, since in Spinoza's God all the attributes work together and are of equal rank, all the other infinitely many attributes must, without our knowing it, be in us men along with the two. According to this doctrine, man is a part of the divine substance, God's nearness is identity with us. (2) But then we find that Spinoza radically denies substantial

Being to man as to all other modes and interpret this unsubstantial "mo-
dality" of man as absolute remoteness from God.

The two views seem to contradict each other. On the one hand, Spinoza
negates the infinite difference between God and man, and on the other, he
degrades man to the level of an unsubstantial mode, lacking the natural
spontaneity of an independent being.

Such objections, which can be found in any number of variations, turn
Spinoza's concepts into an objectively determined apparatus, a model. The
meaning of the concepts is lost. For the only plausible interpretation is
that they designate an intuitive insight, expressed in the medium of rationality but finding its fulfillment and verification in the higher realm of
knowledge.

B. *Human and divine thinking*

The vast difference between divine thought and human thought is that
human thought, because of its origin in a determinate mode, can attain
only to two of God's attributes. "In order to understand something that is
not contained in the deepest foundations of our knowledge, a man's mind
would have to be far higher and more excellent than the human mind."

Our knowledge of the modes in the world is also related to God but not
divine. God thinks the infinite in an infinite way. Man thinks the finite in a
finite way. But although the human mind is not part of the divine substance,
it is nevertheless a part of God's infinite understanding, of the infinite mode.
When we understand something, we say that our idea comes from God,
"not insofar as He is infinite, but insofar as He is manifested through the
nature of the human mind." We say, further, that God has this idea insofar
as He, concurrently with the human mind, also has the idea of another
thing. But this means that the human mind understands this other thing
only partially or inadequately.

C. *Man is mind and body*

Like all things, so also "the essence of man is grounded in certain modifications of God's attributes."

Cogitatio and *extensio*, thought and extension (taken over from Descartes,
not as substances, but as attributes of substance), mark the evident difference
between inwardness and outwardness. They are not two beings: mind (or
soul) and body. Rather, they are one thing in two aspects; one is never
present without the other. This is true of all things. All bodies have mind,
all minds have body. At any one time our knowledge can be directed only
toward one of the two aspects, the mind or the body. But through the inner

structure of the one aspect it discerns the corresponding structure of the other.

Spinoza leaves no doubt as to the unity of mind and body. The actual existence of the human mind, he says, is grounded in the idea of an actually existing particular thing. And the object of this idea, in which the human mind is grounded, is the body or a certain actually existing mode of extension. ("But the human mind or the idea of the human body" expresses no other attributes of God besides the two attributes, thought and extension.) Mind and body are accordingly "one and the same thing, conceived at one time under the attribute of thought, and at another under that of existence."

These statements make it very clear that mind and body are two aspects of the same thing but that there is an unbridgeable difference between them: mind and body cannot act upon one another; the mind and body are both closed systems, each with its own causal relationships, but the two coincide— "The body cannot determine the mind to thought, neither can the mind determine the body to motion or rest." At every moment, to be sure, we are convinced by our immediate action that at a mere sign from the mind the body sometimes moves and sometimes rests. But: "Nobody knows by what means or by what method the mind moves the body." We do not know how what we think we are doing at any moment comes about. But, according to Spinoza's fundamental principle, what in the body seems to be caused by the mind can and must have its ground in the body itself. The immediate experience, in which we suppose our mind to be moving our body, does not carry our knowledge one step further. In investigating ourselves as what we are, as a mode, we can proceed only within one or the other aspect, the mind or the body. To mix the two is confusing for knowledge and fruitless. In investigating the modes, we must remain within one or the other aspect; we must explain all bodily phenomena by the body and all mental phenomena by the mind.

If it is argued that those bodily phenomena which are clearly understandable as effects of the mind cannot be explained on the basis of their bodily causes, Spinoza answers: No one has thus far determined what the body can do, that is, what it can do merely in accordance with the laws of nature, insofar as nature is regarded as purely corporal. No one knows the body so thoroughly as to explain all its functions. "The structure of the human body exceeds in artifice anything that human art has ever constructed." And finally: "In animals we often observe an acuteness of the senses far superior to that of human beings." Thus when people say that this or that action of the body springs from the mind, they do not know what they are saying. They are merely admitting in high-sounding words that they do not know the true cause of an action and that this does not surprise them. But merely by acting in accordance with the laws of nature, a body can do many things at which the mind is amazed when it sees them. Such inquiry, which seeks to explain everything connected with man's body—such as speech, the production of works that are manifested corporeally, or a man's bodily reaction to a piece of devastating news—can go on endlessly. In view of the endless possibilities of our knowledge and of the fundamental coincidence of extension and thought (or, in man, of body and mind), we cannot tell what progress can still be made toward an organic explanation of the phenomena of life, which will throw light on this bodily aspect that today is only seemingly understood as an effect of the mind.

It seems absurd to look for a bodily explanation for what is understandable to us as thought, but must be manifested bodily in order to become real. But Spinoza would reply: Understanding in terms of thought applies only to the aspect of the mind, not to that of the body. It is impossible to understand bodily phenomena by interpreting them as signs in a context of thought. We can investigate only within one or the other aspect, under one or the other attribute. Any inquiry that shuttles back and forth between one domain and the other ends in confusion.

Here one cannot but ask: If mind and body are two aspects of the one, should not this one entity that unites them both be investigated? But this one thing does not exist separately or before or after, as an independent object of investigation. The unity of body and soul is true only as fundamental philosophical knowledge; considered as an object of investigation, it is an illusion. Spinoza conceives of our mind-body unity as a mode in God but is not concerned with man as an anthropological reality.

Here it is not our task to consider the scientific methods of modern psychology and to address critical questions to Spinoza from that vantage point: To what degree is the separation of the two aspects sound and fruitful for investigation? At what point do they cease to be instruments of psychological inquiry? What methods are there that leave the difference out of account, not because they apprehend a substantial unity of body and soul which is in fact inaccessible, but because they envisage concrete phenomena which are at once mental and bodily (expression, language, etc.), or because they deal with facts in which the differentiation disappears (enumeration of actions)? A world of innumerable methods and psychological objects (in Spinoza's usage, modes) has opened up. Spinoza is in need of amplification. But critical scientific research requires an awareness of its methods and limits. This means that such research must remain open toward the realm to which it can never attain. It is from this realm that Spinoza speaks.

In differentiating mind and body in their unity, Spinoza's speculation pursues a practical aim. He rejects all calumny of the body. He says that "the human body, as we feel it, exists." He neither despises nor glorifies the body. He approves neither an attitude of ascetic violence toward it, nor devotion to the body as the only reality. He recognizes neither a disembodied will of the mind nor a mindless body. He sees the unity of the two, which is grounded in the unity of God's substance.

To sum up: Philosophically, we know the unity of body and soul only in Being as a whole. Man is not a substantial part of God, he is not substance. For man is not a source; only God is the source. In considering the mind and body of man, the thinker looks toward the ground in God, but not toward a substance in man. Spinoza goes beyond man, in order to arrive at a fundamental understanding of man.

We remain modes and are in God; that is, we are finite modes within the infinite modes, namely, within the infinite intellect (corresponding to the attribute of thought) and in "motion and rest," corresponding to the attribute of extension. To be sure, we know philosophically that the order and context of corporeal things are the same as the order and context of ideas. But our actual knowledge of the modes is always directed either at the modes of the attribute of extension (at the motion and rest of bodies) or at the modes of the attribute of thought (intellect and will). We do not know the one through the other; we know no effect of one on the other, and assuredly we have no knowledge of a process, whose two aspects would correspond to the inwardness of thought and the outwardness of extension.

D. *Man and animal and the difference among men*

Since according to Spinoza all things in this world of modes are at once mind and body, man takes his place in the scale of natural beings. The gradations are explained as follows: "In proportion as one body is better adapted than another to do or suffer many things, in the same proportion will the mind at the same time be better adapted to perceive many things, and the more the actions of a body depend upon itself alone, and the less other bodies co-operate with it in action, the better adapted will the mind be for directly understanding." Thus far there is no fundamental difference, but only a difference in degree, between the divers modes and hence between man and other beings. But the difference between animal and man is nevertheless radical for Spinoza, for man can think and therefore has affects whose nature is rooted in thinking. This distinction results in an equally radical difference between man's attitude toward other men and toward beasts. Sound reason "teaches us to unite in friendship with men, and not with brutes, nor with things whose nature is different from human nature." We have the same right over the animals as they over us. Spinoza does not deny that animals have feelings. But we have a right to use "them for our own pleasure and treat them as is most convenient for us, inasmuch as they do not agree in nature with us, and their affects are different from our own."

The hallmark of man is that he knows that he knows; he has reason. The more rational he is, the freer he is, the more real, the more perfect. Here the question arises: "Why did God not create men in such a way that they would be governed only by the guidance of reason?" Answer: "Because He did not lack the matter with which to make everything from the highest to the lowest degree of perfection, or, to speak more accurately, because the laws of nature were so all-embracing that they sufficed to produce everything that could be understood by an infinite intellect."

Everything arises of necessity, in accordance with God's eternal laws. This applies equally to the actions of the pious, that is, of those who have a clear idea of God, by which all their thoughts and actions are determined, and to the godless, that is, those who do not possess an idea of God, but merely ideas of the earthly things by which their thoughts and actions are determined. The acts of these two groups are different not in degree but in content. Within the necessary consequences of God's substance, in the infinite universe of nature, there is a natural necessity, which is the necessity of a rational life. But what diversities there are among men and nations, only experience can tell us. It teaches that men of authentic reason, philosophers, are rare. It teaches that some peoples are freedom-loving and others servile. This diversity becomes an essential element in Spinoza's political thinking.

It may be asked: Does the imperfect exist because everything that is possible should exist? In other words, does it exist for the sake of the richest possible diversity, and not of the good? Or in order that there should be an unbroken scale from best to worst, in which everything occurs and has its place? Spinoza gives but one answer: Everything follows necessarily from God. The evaluations, however, spring from the mind of man. Eternal necessity is beyond good and evil, beauty and ugliness.

B. *Immortality and eternity*

The soul, Spinoza writes in the early *Treatise,* has the choice of uniting with the body, whose idea it is, or with God, without whom it cannot subsist or be conceived of. If it is united only with the body, it must die with the body. But if it unites with something that is immutable and enduring, it will necessarily endure with it. This is what happens when the soul unites with God; then it is reborn in knowing love of God. For its first birth was to be united with the body; in the second birth, we experience the effects not of the body but of love, which corresponds to the knowledge of that incorporeal object.

This line of thought is made clearer in the *Ethics* by the distinction between immortality as duration and eternity as timeless existence. The body-soul unit is utterly mortal. Only as long as the body endures can the soul imagine anything and remember things past. Thus it is not possible for us to remember that we existed before the body: "Only insofar, therefore, as it involves the actual existence of the body can the mind be said to possess duration, and its existence be limited by a fixed time, and so far only has it the power of determining the existence of things in time, and of conceiving them under the form of duration." Thus, inevitably, "the present existence of the mind and its power to form ideas are annulled as soon as the mind ceases to affirm the present existence of the body."

Nevertheless we feel ourselves to be eternal, "for demonstrations are the eyes of the mind by which it sees and observes things." Although we do not remember having existed before the body, we feel that our mind, insofar as it knows and encompasses the nature of the body under the form of eternity, is removed from time. Hence "the human mind cannot be absolutely destroyed with the body, but something of it remains which is eternal."

But this "eternity cannot be defined by time, or have any relationship to it." True immortality cannot be understood in terms of time and duration. The opinion of men, who are rightly conscious of the eternity of the mind, confuses it with duration. "They impute eternity to the faculty of forming ideas or to the memory, supposing them to endure after death."

Immortality, which is not duration in time but eternity, cannot encompass what is purely temporal. Hence it can be imputed only to that which is "conceived under the form of eternity" and which in thought is experienced as a participation in eternity. Knowledge of the third and highest variety knows the eternal and is itself eternal. "No other love is eternal than spiritual love." The unity of mind and body signifies, however, that the body is not nothing or doomed to vanish into nothingness, but ceases to be only in its variable aspect. "In God there necessarily exists an idea which expresses the essence of this or that body under some form of eternity" and so enables what is a temporal figure in the successive ages of life to subsist timelessly in eternity. Spinoza insisted with equal force on the transience of the mind's bodily existence and on the eternity of its essence.

In bodily existence we are subject to affects, hence to fear of death. But as naturally rational beings we free ourselves through knowledge from affects, including the fear of death, and attain the peace of eternal Being, to which we already and at all times belong. The brighter our rational insight and concomitantly the power of our love, the more perfectly we attain to it. In our existence as modes, we remain imprisoned in inadequate ideas, in a limited faculty of knowledge. But in this same existence we, as rational beings, gain adequate ideas, though they are always limited. With them we partake of that Being which, in our immediate relationship to God, in God, in substance, we ascertain through thought. By thinking, we pass from existence as a mode to the Being of substance. We ourselves do not become substance, but we belong to it as a mode of its attributes. In principle this is so of all things, but only in rational beings is it so by virtue of their own knowledge and the inner attitude corresponding to this knowledge.

From the standpoint of corporeal existence in time, the desire of all things to assert their existence is the passion to go on living as long as possible. But in the ground of this existence there speaks the certainty of eternal being, unrelated to duration, memory, imagination; this certainty is elucidated in thought.

VI. FREEDOM FROM AIMS AND VALUES

A. *Purposes and values are prejudices arising from a perversion of the idea of God*

"We can be more certain of the existence of no thing than of the existence of the absolutely infinite or perfect being, that is, of God." But it is Spinoza's perpetual concern that this idea of God should not be perverted, that God should not be degraded and sullied by our imaginations. If the idea of God becomes false, all judgments become false.

The pure idea of God implies His necessary existence. He exists and acts solely by the necessity of His nature. He is the free cause of all things. Everything is in God, so that without Him it can neither be nor be understood. Everything is predetermined by God, not, however, through an arbitrary choice, but through God's unconditioned nature or infinite power.

This idea of God is obscured by men's prejudices, which all in turn spring from one prejudice: the common assumption that all things act, like men, for a purpose. Thus men suppose that God guides everything toward a definite end; that God created all things for the sake of man and man in order that man might worship Him.

The source of this human prejudice is that all men come into the world without knowledge of the causes of things and that they all seek their profit, that is, they act for a purpose and are conscious of this drive in themselves. Accordingly, they look upon everything in nature as a means to their own profit, and when they find something useful that they themselves have not produced, they believe that another being of their own kind has made it for their benefit. Their understanding of things is based on the utility of these things to themselves, hence on final causes. Consequently they do not inquire into their own cause. This prejudice turns to superstition when men meet with harmful things, such as storms, earthquakes, disease. They imagine that the gods who have made things for their benefit are angry because men have offended them. They cast about for ways of pleasing the gods. Believing that the gods provide useful things in order to obligate men and so receive their highest veneration, men have devised different ways of worshiping God, each group in the hope that He will love them more than all others. They imagine the gods and nature to be as insane as they themselves. And this conception is not corrected by the daily experience that useful and harmful things come in equal measure to those who perform such superstitious worship and to those who do not. They cling to their deep-rooted prejudice, saying that the judgments of the gods are far beyond human understanding.

Spinoza opposes such prejudice with the conviction, supported and elucidated by his whole philosophy, that all final causes are nothing but human imagination. Everything in nature happens with eternal necessity and supreme perfection. God acts, but has no purpose. For He needs no other. There is nothing that He lacks.

Although Spinoza denies the "purpose" in Being, he understands purposive thinking in human existence as a part of man's situation of finiteness and deficiency. In the substance of being, in God, there is no deficiency, hence no purpose. Nor has nature any purposes. All natural reality is free not only from purposes but from values. Spinoza shows how we transfer our value judgments to nature, as though values were given objectively in nature: A man intends to build a house. If it is not yet finished, the builder will say it is imperfect. Once universal models of houses have been conceived, structures are judged according to the degree to which they correspond to such models. In the same way, men form universal ideas of natural things, which they look upon as models, and when things in nature do not agree with such ideas they say that nature has blundered. Good and evil are not positive properties of things; they are modes of thought.

By transferring their judgments of things to Being itself, men color the world with values that are unrelated to its intrinsic reality. But though Spinoza denies the independent existence of values, he recognizes them as modes of thought in our limited existence.

The deformation of God into a purposive, hence deficient being, who obligates men, benefits them, or is angry with them, who allows Himself to be influenced by men's acts and devotions, results in a distorted view of everything. For values are thus removed from the perspective of a being who exists as a mode circumscribed by time and space and desires His profit, and transformed into things endowed with objective, independent, and absolute existence, which are called by such names as good and evil, order and confusion, beauty and ugliness, virtue and vice. But any such perspective is alien to God. To transfer it to God is to remove God's sublimity from the view of reason.

Only in our limited perspective do we suppose that we find an order in things themselves. For, because it is easier and hence pleasant, we prefer order to confusion, as though there were an order in nature apart from its relation to our faculty of thought. The prejudice is not dispelled by the knowledge that there are infinitely many things which far surpass our understanding, and many things that confuse our feeble powers of thought. Even certain philosophers, Spinoza observes, are convinced that the movements of the heavenly bodies form a harmony. Each one, in Spinoza's opinion, views things according to the constitution of his own mind. That is why there are so many controversies among men, and the final outcome is skepticism. Everything goes to show that men prefer to imagine things than to know them. But modes of imagining do not disclose the nature of any thing; all they show is the state of our imagination.

Only a perversion of the idea of God leads to the notion of theodicy (the supposed justification of God in the face of the supposed evil, wickedness, and misery of the world). "What then is the source of so much imperfection in nature, of the stench and putrefaction of things, their loathsome misshapenness, of confusion, evil, crime, etc.?" Spinoza answers by denying that this evil state of affairs is true in an absolute sense. It exists only in the imagination of modal beings, who, in their drive to assert themselves in this world, judge things, with their finite intelligence, according to the criterion of usefulness to man.

But this mode of thought is itself necessary and understandable because man is a mode, a finite being. Thus Spinoza describes the finiteness, limitation, and confusion of man's modal existence.

B. *Our limited intelligence*

We need not be wholly dominated by our limited state of being, for as thinking beings we know it, understand it, and can thereby rise above it. Spinoza clarifies by comparisons what pure thought has revealed to him concerning our state.

He compares our state with that of a fictitious worm in the blood stream, which has the faculty of sight in order to differentiate the components of the blood, and reason in order to observe how they act upon one another. "This little worm would live in the blood as we live in this part of the universe." It would observe the blood but fail to notice that our movements and other outward modifications affect the blood as a whole. We are compelled to understand all natural bodies in the same way as this worm does the blood. But because the nature of the universe is not limited like the nature of the blood, but absolutely infinite, each particle is governed in an infinite way and compelled to suffer infinite modifications. Thus the human body is a part of infinite nature and likewise the human mind, namely of the infinite mode of thought. The infinite intellect (*intellectus infinitus*) contains all nature objectively within itself. The human mind is this same power, but only as a finite part of the infinite mind. Hence it does not understand infinite nature any more than it is itself infinite. We can, to be sure, acquire the conviction that every part of nature is related to the whole. But we remain in ignorance as to *how* the whole and every part accord with the whole. For "to know this it would be necessary to know all nature and all its parts."

Spinoza offers another comparison for the way in which we pursue our purpose. "Bees store up provisions for the winter, but man, who is over them, who raises them and cares for them, has an entirely different purpose, namely to keep the honey for himself. Thus man, insofar as he is a particular being, has no purpose other than that which his limited nature can attain, but insofar as he is at the same time a part and instrument of nature as a whole, each of man's purposes cannot be the ultimate purpose of nature, for nature is infinite and makes use of him as of all others as its instrument."

The comparison of man with the fictitious worm in the blood refers to his limited knowledge in this part of the world and in the infinite universe. The comparison of man with the bees refers to the "ultimate purpose of nature," which elsewhere Spinoza does not call purpose, but purposeless necessity. In relation to this natural purpose, man can only be a subordinate instrument, whose purposes are mere means for the great superior power, which destroys them by making use of them; just as man's transient existence remains subordinate to the cosmos and does not govern it. But this whole perspective of purpose is rooted in finite conceptions. Spinoza drops it and effects the leap to universal freedom from purpose.

Both comparisons are attempts to disclose the situation of our modal existence and so overcome anthropocentric thinking. Spinoza's great intuition of the infinite world as the infinite mode of substance implies on the one hand that man, bound to his modal existence, is vanishingly small, but on the other hand that he is great by virtue of his reason, which renders him capable of this intuition. Man's knowledge of his limitation is itself a factor in the beatitude of being-in-God, which this knowledge makes possible.

c. *Reality and value*

To evaluate reality, to glorify one reality and to deplore or indignantly reject another, is for Spinoza a sign of confinement in modal existence. But Spinoza himself is constantly evaluating things (and particularly man) as more or less perfect. He overcomes this contradiction by equating perfection and reality ("By reality and perfection I understand the same thing") and by the thesis that there are degrees of reality equivalent to greater or lesser perfection. Value is graduated reality.

Here Spinoza has taken over an ancient concept of reality. In his view, empirical things in space and time either have reality or have not, they are without degrees of reality, but the reality of substantiality in the modes is graduated. Thus from different standpoints Spinoza can say: "All happening in nature is supremely perfect." But on the other hand: "That effect is the most perfect which is immediately produced by God, and a thing is imperfect in proportion as intermediate causes are necessary for its production."

The reason for the perfection of things is not that they "delight or offend the senses of men, or that they appeal to or antagonize human nature," but lies solely in their "nature and force." In reality, "perfection and imperfection are only modes of thought; that is to say, notions which we are in the habit of forming from the comparison with one another of individuals of the same species or genus." But such a comparison is not based on the relation of these individuals to our purpose. It shows, rather, that some individuals "possess more Being or reality than others—insofar do we call some more perfect than others; and insofar as we assign to the latter anything which, like limitation, termination, impotence, involves negation, shall we call them imperfect."

This difference of value, which is always a difference in degree of reality, power, proximity to God, lies in ourselves and our ideas: "One idea is more valuable than another and contains more reality, according as the object of the one is more valuable than the object of the other and contains more reality." "The farther a man has advanced in this class of knowledge, the more conscious he is of himself and of God, that is, the more perfect he is."

Thus Spinoza's view of the identity of reality and value is twofold in its consequences; on the one hand there are no values, but on the other hand, value judgments are repeatedly put forward, on the supposition that they apply to degrees of reality.

D. *The shift from one class of knowledge to another*

We have two related kinds of knowledge: an immediate knowledge of God by the intellect, and a mediated knowledge of Him through the other modes. In immediate knowledge, philosophical thought is turned freely toward God's infinity and filled with it; in its mediated relation to the modes, finite knowledge is unfree and limited. For, being finite, it is unable to encompass the infinity of the modes, and can only go forward endlessly, while remaining ignorant of the whole.

Because man is a finite mode which lives amid bodily affects, but is at the same time a rational being that loves God, Spinoza's sentences contain a persistent contradiction (which can be overcome only by the differentiation of the second and third classes of knowledge).

In line with his fundamental idea, Spinoza is constantly effecting a shift which the reader finds disturbing at first, but which then seems to confirm the truth of the whole: from purposive thinking to freedom from purposes; from value judgments to the valueless intuition of necessity; from the demand for activity to the perfect peace that comes of leaving all things as they are.

These shifts of viewpoint can also be interpreted the other way around: from God's purposeless eternity to an understanding of purposive thinking as a limitation of thought in modal existence; from a value-free intuition of the totality to an understanding of the relativity of false valuations; from peace in the certainty of God to the activity of man as a mode; from eternal, divine necessity in which there is no "ought" to the ought of determinate human laws.

In metaphysical terms, the shift is in one case an ascending movement from the modes to substance, and in the other the descending movement from substance to modes. But in the modes lies the expression of substance itself.

E. *The ethos of freedom from values*

"I shall consider human actions and appetites just as if I were considering lines, planes, or bodies." "Most persons who have written about the affects . . . attribute the cause of human weakness and changeableness, not to the common power of nature, but to some vice of human nature, which they therefore bewail, laugh at, mock, or . . . detest. . . . [But] nothing happens in nature which can be attributed to any vice in nature." In the *Political Treatise* he repeats: "I have labored carefully not to mock, lament, or execrate, but to understand human actions; and to this end I have looked upon passions, such as love, hatred, envy, ambition, pity and the other perturbations of the mind, not in the light of vices of human nature, but as properties, just as pertinent to it, as are heat, cold, storm, thunder, and the like, which phenomena, though inconvenient, are yet necessary, and have fixed causes."

Spinoza envisages an attitude "beyond good and evil." He does not wish to condemn, to judge, to appraise, for he takes the philosophical attitude implied by knowledge of God. If everything happens according to the eternal laws, according to God's necessity, it becomes possible to view events as Spinoza viewed two spiders that he had put into the same net, watching them fight until one had enmeshed, killed, and eaten the other. But in this attitude, two elements are involved: devotion to God's necessity and striving for the truth of objective scientific knowledge, which suspends all value judgments and purposes in order to apprehend things in their pure objectivity.

What Galileo inaugurated in the natural sciences when he contested the

pre-eminent rank that had hitherto been accorded to spheres and circles, and what Max Weber completed in the humanities when he showed how value judgments could be investigated without recourse to values, would have met with Spinoza's approval. But Spinoza had much more in mind: not only a suspension of one's own evaluations during the hours of investigation and every moment of objective judgment, but an inward and general attitude of mind, in which value judgments are not only suspended for a limited time, but transcended as a whole: the affirmation of everything that is, because it follows from God's necessity in accordance with the laws of nature.

It is valid to ask whether there is an inner relationship between the greatness and force of the idea of God and the possibility of a science truly free from value judgments, and the question can be answered in the affirmative. Nevertheless, we are dealing with two different things on two different planes when we speak of overcoming the value judgments which becloud our objective knowledge of things in the world, and of overcoming the perverted view of God which arises when our God-given serenity is disturbed by notions of theodicy.

VII. SERVITUDE AND FREEDOM OF MIND

Spinoza's fundamental intuition that Being is free from purposes and that our true knowledge is free from values has two consequences: first, it enables us to understand the servitude to purposes and value judgments imposed on man by his affects; and second, it shows the way leading out of his servitude to freedom. But this freedom is nothing other than insight. Put into practice, the fundamental intuition is itself freedom.

Accordingly, Spinoza does two things: casting off all values, he investigates the affects and the necessary conditions of their origin, relationships, and process—and then, by a reversal, effects the most radical philosophical evaluation; he considers the highest good and examines everything accordingly as it promotes or obstructs this highest good. As consciousness of necessity, philosophy investigates the nature of things. As life practice, philosophy subordinates itself to the idea of the highest good.

Spinoza knows this. After saying that good and evil are not in things themselves, but are only modes in our thinking, he continues: "But although things are so . . . we must retain these words . . . since we desire to form for ourselves an idea of man upon which we may look as a model of human nature." Consequently, he calls good what is a means of coming closer to the model of human nature that we set before us; and evil, what prevents us from approaching it. And men will be termed more or less perfect according as they come more or less close to the model.

From a state in which man's mind is determined at every step by purposes and values, it attains, through a reversal in its understanding of "purpose," to the highest good. To deny the existence of purposes is not to renounce the will to reason.

Thus Spinoza rejects all ideas of purpose purporting to convey an understanding of being, but allows of preference, choice, evaluation in man's quest of salvation as the rational good. Or in other words: in respect of human affairs, Spinoza leaves room for value judgments; in respect of the totality, he does not. But this freedom from values can be attained only by a process of evaluation.

Thus despite Spinoza's rejection of values, he speaks of the "right mode of life," of "decrees of reason," of the "highest good." The contradiction is not solved by the possibility of choosing one's way of life arbitrarily. Quite the contrary, the highest good also springs *necessarily,* in the nature of things, from reason. The evaluation that occurs on the way to it is a factor in the all-embracing reality that must be regarded as free from values. But what distinguishes the highest good from all other goods and values is that as the ultimate purpose it ceases to be a purpose. Not only does it serve no other purpose, but, insofar as it is willed, it is already present. It is not willed as something else; rather the will to it, reason, is itself. The highest good is present in rational thought, which is always at the same time action. It cannot be intended unless in a certain sense it has already been attained.

The crucial problem is freedom. The contradiction in Spinoza seems unbridgeable. He denies freedom and asserts it. His whole philosophy is based on freedom. In thought and work and practice, his ethos aims at the promotion of freedom. The solution lies in the different meaning of freedom.

On the one hand: There is no freedom. Everything is necessary. Spinoza explains why freedom of the will is self-deception: "Created things are all determined from without. From an external cause a stone receives a certain quantum of motion. The stone's perseverance in motion is necessary, because it is determined by the impact of the external cause. . . . Now let us imagine that the stone thinks while continuing to move, and knows itself to be striving to remain as far as possible in motion. This stone will certainly be of the opinion that it is perfectly free and persists in motion only because it so wills. Such is the human freedom of whose possession all are so proud; all it signifies, however, is that men are conscious of their desire, but do not know the causes by which they are determined. Thus a child thinks itself free when it desires milk, a boy when in anger he desires revenge, a fearful person when he wishes to run away. Even a drunken man supposes that he speaks from free choice. . . . And since this prejudice is innate in all men, they do not easily free themselves of it."

On the other hand: There is freedom. But what does Spinoza mean by freedom? Freedom is one with necessity. A distinction is made between necessity by outward compulsion, or external cause, and necessity as action in inner obedience to one's own nature. Where the action results purely from the consequences of one's own essence, this necessity is at the same time the most perfect freedom. This perfect freedom belongs only to God. God's freedom is not free will, but free cause; it is not choice, but perfect self-determination, "free necessity." "God acts from the laws of His own nature only, and is compelled by no one." "God alone exists from the necessity alone of His own nature and acts from the necessity alone of His own nature. Therefore He alone is a free cause."

It is different with the modes, with men. Man is free only insofar as he is the adequate cause of his action in clear knowledge of its cause and effect. But he is unfree insofar as he thinks and acts on the basis of inadequate ideas, moved by affects from inside and outside, in the endless interaction of the modes. Since man in his existence as a whole is never, in the lucidity of adequate ideas, the sole and complete cause, he is always unfree.

But even if man is not perfectly free, he can become freer by conceiving adequate ideas, that is, by becoming rational. In reason he knows necessity. Consequently, there is no freedom, everything is necessary; but man's insight into the necessity of his own essence is itself freedom, for freedom is knowing participation in necessity. The will to freedom, which is identical with the will to knowledge, understands itself as necessity. Freedom consists in looking upon all things and events as necessary, in understanding even value judgments and purposive thinking as conditioned by the necessity of modal being; finally, freedom is the self-understanding of reason as the necessary nature of man.

Spinoza's conception of freedom and necessity is complicated by the notion of an "ought." The moral law ordains something that does not necessarily happen, but can also not happen. According to Spinoza, there are two kinds of laws: those which determine the invariable course of things, and those which are norms according to which men should, but do not always, act. We ordinarily suppose that our freedom resides in our ability to follow the moral law or not. What Spinoza means by freedom is first made clear by his conception of law: only laws that cannot be transgressed are divine; those that can be transgressed are human. Freedom consists in union with divine necessity; it acts without choice. Where I choose but might act otherwise, I am unfree.

The laws of men are an expression of their finiteness. "All laws that can be transgressed are human laws, because when men decide something for their own good, it does not follow that this thing will redound to the good of nature as a whole; on the contrary, it may bring about the destruction of many other things." But more powerful than the laws of men are the laws of nature, to which the former in turn are subordinated.

The contradiction between freedom and necessity is thus resolved by the following view: The moral law is situated within necessity; here necessity elucidates itself and understands itself as such, or, in Spinoza's words, it is not incurred but enacted. For adequate knowledge is identical with action, not with passivity. It is realization of the soul in accordance with divine necessity. Achieved through thought, freedom is an actively self-conscious element of divine, all-embracing, absolute necessity.

But to suppose that God promulgates laws like men, that He rewards obedience and punishes disobedience to these laws, is one of the false notions that spring from the transference of human action and human limitation to God. It is first of all a diminution of God, for everything that happens happens really and irresistibly in accordance with His own decision, and nothing can be done in opposition to Him. Moreover, the idea of a reward corrupts moral virtue: for virtue has its reward in itself, not in something else.

In many of its formulations, Spinoza's necessity resembles Calvin's predestination, although the origin of Spinoza's idea and the inner attitude that follows from it are entirely different. Spinoza writes: "No one is justified in finding fault with God for giving him a weak nature or an impotent mind. This would be as absurd as if a circle were to complain that God had not given it the properties of a sphere." "Men are unpardonable before God if only for the reason that they are in God's power, as clay in the hands of a potter, who from the same mass makes vessels, the ones to His honor, the others to His dishonor." Against Spinoza it may be argued here that if man is necessarily as he is, he is pardonable. Spinoza answers: "Men can always be pardonable and nevertheless want for happiness and be tormented in many ways."

Spinoza has a certain inclination to Calvinism. He writes that the view that everything depends on God's judgment is closer to the truth than the opinion that God does everything with a view to the good. For this latter view assumes the existence of something outside of God, which does not depend on Him, but to which He looks as to a model. "In practice this is to subordinate God to blind fate." But there is a radical difference between Spinoza and Calvin: Spinoza knows no preference on the part of God, no arbitrary decision, no "*decretum horribile*," but only necessity. But a more profound difference is to be found in the very core of their doctrine: in Calvin, consciousness of sin and the need of redemption through faith; in Spinoza, fundamental freedom from all consciousness of guilt or sin and the peace bestowed by freedom grounded in the certainty of God.

A. *The theory of the affects*

Spinoza reduces the operation of the affects to a few simple principles, which explain the highly diversified varieties. Since antiquity there had been a traditional doctrine of the affects, which at Spinoza's time had been renewed and transformed, especially by Descartes and Malebranche. Spinoza knew the tradition. "But no one, so far as I know, has determined the nature and strength of the affects, and what the mind is able to do toward controlling them."

The third book of the *Ethics* deals with the origin and nature of the affects. It has become famous. Johannes Müller, a great physiologist, regarded this section as an unexcelled analysis of the affects and included the whole of it in his *Handbook of Physiology* (1833-40).

The fundamental principles are as follows:

1. All finite modes produce each other, help and destroy one another. No thing can be destroyed by itself. Rather, each thing strives *to endure in being* for an indeterminate time. The striving for self-preservation is the real essence of each thing and also of man.

Spinoza calls the striving for self-preservation *desire* when it is conscious of itself and *appetite* when it is not. According to the aspect in which it is considered, it also has many other names. Accordingly, says Spinoza, "it combines all the strivings of human nature, which we designate by the names appetite, will, desire, or impulse."

Striving is *motion*. But motion is based on a state of the finite essence. Spinoza calls the *state* of the human essence affection (whether the state is innate or acquired, conceived under the attribute of thought or that of extension, or related to both at once). Desire (or endeavor, appetite, volition) can differ according to the state of the same man, or it may even take an opposite course, so that the man is drawn in different directions and does not know which way to turn.

2. The transition to greater reality in perfection is equivalent to the affect of *joy*; the transition to lesser reality or perfection is equivalent to the affect of *sorrow*. The affect resides in transition. "If a man were born with the perfection to which he passes, he would possess it without the affect of joy." Sorrow is also in transition. In a permanent state of lesser perfection it ceases.

3. "I acknowledge only three primary affects, those of joy, sorrow, and desire . . . The others spring from these."

What gives rise to these affects? The mind represents *objects*, which govern the movement of the affects. In relation to the striving for self-preservation, all objects take on a coloration of the advantageous or disadvantageous. "We neither strive for, wish, seek, nor desire anything because we adjudge it to be good, but, on the contrary, we adjudge a thing to be good because we strive for, wish, seek, or desire it."

The mind strives to represent what will increase the effectiveness of the mind-body totality, and resists the contrary representations. Thence result the first fundamental, objectively determined affects: *love* and *hate*. Love is joy, accompanied by the idea of an external cause. Hate is sorrow, accompanied by the idea of an external cause.

All our experience is interrelated. There is, for example, a temporal relationship: we may love or hate a thing merely because we have considered it while experiencing an affect of joy or sorrow that it did not bring about. Similarities between things produce the same result. Thus we can hate and love the same thing, and our state of mind often fluctuates.

The affects are also determined in relation to representations of past and future things. A "pang of conscience" is sorrow, accompanied by the idea of a past thing that happened unexpectedly. Fear and hope, which are inseparable, are sorrow and joy accompanied by the representation of a future thing—when the vacillation ceases, the result is certainty or despair. Here it will not be possible to reproduce the whole of Spinoza's penetrating analysis of the affects.

4. The principal dividing line between the affects is created by the difference between *adequate* and *inadequate ideas*. Desire (striving for self-assertion) and joy and sorrow are either actions or passions (active or passive). The mind experiences joy in adequate ideas, through which it is active, experiences sorrow in inadequate ideas, through which it is passive. In both cases the fundamental striving is the will to remain in being; in the one case, clearly and rationally, in the other, confusedly and blindly.

Rational striving results in mastery over the affects, or freedom; confused and blind striving brings servitude to the affects, or bondage.

B. *Description of bondage*

The situation of all finite modes including man is characterized by the fact that there is no individual thing in nature to which some other individual thing is not superior in power. There is always something more powerful. Hence the power with which a man perseveres in existence is limited and infinitely exceeded by the power of external causes.

Instead of adequate ideas, he has confused representations which indicate more the present state of the human body than the nature of an object outside it. These representations (as, for example, of the size and distance of the sun) do not conflict with the truth and do not disappear in its presence. Representations are not dispelled because the truth is present, but because they are opposed by more powerful representations.

If man incurred only changes that could be understood on the basis of his own nature, he would not pass away but would exist forever, he would be infinite. But he is finite, exposed to external forces. He follows the common order of nature, that is, he exists necessarily not only through his actions, but is always necessarily subject to the "passions," or affects.

The growth and the duration of every passion are determined by the power of the external cause in proportion to our own power. A passion, or affect, can so exceed all a man's other actions as to cling to him permanently. Affects can only be resisted and eliminated by other, opposed and more powerful affects. Consequently, an affect can be resisted by a true knowledge of good and evil when this knowledge itself takes the form of an affect.

Things present have greater power than those that are absent. An affect relating to something that is immediately present in space and time is more powerful than one relating to something that is swiftly approaching or to something that is far removed from our actuality. That is why an opinion produced by an object that stands before us is so much more powerful than true reason. As the poet said: "I see the good and approve of it, but I cede to evil."

For Spinoza a man who follows his affect and opinion is "in bondage." One who lives solely in accordance with his reason is free. The former acts without knowing what he is doing. The latter, obedient only to himself, does only what he regards as most important in life and consequently desires most.

c. *The idea and possibility of freedom*

The decrees of reason are grounded in the necessary fact that everyone strives to preserve his being to the best of his ability. Since "all our strivings follow from the necessity of our nature," "the foundation of virtue (*virtus*, power) is that endeavor itself to preserve our own being, and happiness consists in this—that a man can preserve his own being." "To act according to reason is nothing but to do those things which follow from the necessity of our nature." There is no nobler motivation than the striving for self-preservation. "Since reason demands nothing which is opposed to nature, it demands, therefore, that every person should love himself, should seek his own profit." To act according to the guidance of reason, to preserve one's being, to live—these three mean the same thing, to act according to virtue. Spinoza knew himself to be at variance with the prevailing ethical view. "Many suppose that the principle which obliges every man to seek his profit, is the basis of immorality and not of virtue and sense of duty." But the truth, he declares, "is the exact opposite."

It may be argued that there is no need to strive for what will happen in any case according to natural necessity. This seeming paradox in Spinoza is explained by the twofold meaning of nature and necessity, which may be either the unconscious necessity of inadequate ideas or the conscious necessity of adequate ideas. For Spinoza demands that we seek the profit "that is truly profit," that we should not desire blindly, but strive for "what truly leads man to greater perfection," that we should not take finite aims as our ultimate goal, but only reason itself and what is revealed to it.

Spinoza expounds this ethos in three ways: (1) he indicates procedures,

SPINOZA 57

makes recommendations, and sets up rules of life; (2) he recalls over and over again that all truth has its ground and point of reference in the certainty of God; (3) he sets forth a model of the rational life.

1. Procedures and rules of life

It is necessary "to know the strength and weakness of our nature in order to determine what reason can accomplish in mastering the affects and what it cannot accomplish." The notion of a will which on the basis of fixed judgments can subjugate the affects and passions (the Stoics, Descartes) is a delusion. The passions cannot be counteracted by such violence. Only "knowledge of the soul" can help us to determine what measures will be effective.

Spinoza shows that an affect that is a passion ceases to be a passion as soon as we form a clear and distinct idea of it. "Thus the better known an affect is to us the more it is in our power, and the less the soul suffers from it." Everyone has the power to know his affects clearly and distinctly, if not wholly then at least in part, and consequently to suffer less from them. Impulses and desires are passions only insofar as they spring from inadequate ideas; they may all be counted as virtues as soon as they are aroused or created by adequate ideas. In the soul there is no other power than the power to think and to form adequate ideas. In the course of time, clear ideas gain the upper hand over the unclear ideas of the affects.

In thinking I become master of my affects by following certain procedures, which can be clearly elucidated:

I am overpowered by an affect when all my thinking is chained to the external object to which I relate the affect. I become free when I "detach the affect from my thought of its external causes and connect it with other thoughts." Then love and hate of the external cause are extinguished.

I am overwhelmed by blind chance. What has happened to me need not have happened. But once I recognize the necessity of things, I suffer less from my affects and gain power over them. Thus "grief over a lost possession is diminished as soon as the man who has lost the possession considers that he could not have preserved it in any way."

I am taken unawares. Suddenly I am assailed by something that offends, angers, frightens me. To defend myself against it, I must order my affects, that is, project in my mind a sound mode of life or certain rules of conduct, imprint these on my memory, and apply them to every situation that occurs.

Spinoza rejects certain emotions that are generally held in high esteem: *pity*, as such, is evil and useless. A wise man strives not to be moved by pity, for it is a weak affect that weakens. He endeavors, rather, to obey the pure decree of reason in performing the helpful action that he knows to be good. To pity no one, but to do good. He adds, however: "But this I say expressly of the man who lives according to the guidance of reason. For he who is moved neither by reason nor by pity to be of any service to others is properly called inhuman; for he seems to be unlike a man." *Humility* is not a virtue, for it does not spring from reason and is a source of weakness. *Repentance* is not a virtue; one who repents of an action is doubly wretched and weak.

Highly characteristic of Spinoza is his discussion of the theorem: What brings joy is good. In the ordering of our thoughts and representations we should, as far as possible, consider only the good in each thing, in order that the affect of joy should impel us to act. To revile, accuse, despise is not only useless, but results from an unnoticed perversion. The most ambitious of men deplores the vanity of the world when he is unsuccessful. A man forsaken by his loved one reviles the inconstancy of women, but all is forgotten the moment she takes him back. The complaints of those who suffer an adverse fate are an expression of weakness. Hence a man desirous of freedom tries to fill his mind with the joy that comes from a sound knowledge of the virtues and their causes; he will not expend his powers in considering the failings of men, in disparaging men, and in enjoying a false appearance of freedom. He will avoid listing the failings of men and speak only sparingly of human weakness.

But only the joy which is reason itself is good. According to the nature and states of men their joys are very different, as for example the joy of the drunkard and that of the philosopher. The latter is the highest goal. "If a man affected with joy were led to such perfection as to conceive adequately himself and his actions, he would be fitted—better than ever before—for the performance of those actions to which he is now determined by affects which are passions." "The greater the joy with which we are affected, the greater the perfection to which we pass, and consequently the more do we participate in the divine nature."

Opposed to the unique value of joy is the superstitious belief that what causes unhappiness is good. But only an envious man takes pleasure in my helplessness and misfortune. "Nothing but a gloomy and sad superstition forbids enjoyment. . . . No God . . . esteems as any virtue in us tears, sighs, fears . . . ; on the contrary . . . to make use of things and to delight in them as much as possible . . . is the part of a wise man."

2. *All truth relates to God*

Any way of life that does not have its ultimate source in the certainty of God is futile. Thus rules and methods, prescriptions and programs for the conduct of life, are not enough. They may, to be sure, be helpful in showing the way to "right" behavior, but even right behavior draws its meaning and force from the underlying ground. Hence it is not possible to master the confusion of the affects by psychological insight alone, as though operating a machine that responds to specific manipulations.

Spinoza states this idea repeatedly: "The final aim of a man who is guided by reason, that is to say, the chief desire by which he strives to govern all his other desires, is that by which he is led adequately to conceive himself and all things which can be conceived by his intelligence." To conceive adequately is to conceive in the third class of knowledge. But a necessary consequence of this knowledge is the intellectual love of God (*amor intellectualis dei*), "joy, accompanied by the idea of God as its cause." Or rather, this knowledge is itself this love of God. Hence the highest happiness is "the knowledge of God, which leads us to do only what love and the sense of duty demand."

The certainty and power of the consciousness of God's reality, of the all-encompassing, all-permeating reality which is always present to the man who does not close himself to it, has immediate consequences for every day of a man's life. Because God is present, the moral law is real; it is not a product of constraint but springs up as though of itself.

Our entire philosophical endeavor is to attain to God's presence and to return when we have fallen away from it. Always reflecting and aiming in that direction, the mind "can bring it about that all bodily affections or imaginations of things will relate to the idea of God." And the power of this knowledge and love of God "is magnified when we conceive that more and more men are joined with God by the same bond of love."

3. Project of a rational life

Freedom from purpose: Being is wholly present; as love it is eternal presence; it is not somewhere else, not to be looked for and anticipated in another world.

Consequently, the third class of knowledge does not operate as a means to an end, but is itself the end: happiness resides in this *amor intellectualis dei*. It is subservient to nothing else; it is not merely the way to something else, but is itself the goal.

This is essential for an understanding of true virtue: "Blessedness is not the reward of virtue, but is virtue itself." Consequently the rational, ethical life is to be sought after for its own sake, not for the sake of something else. When it is regarded as a means to something else, it ceases to be a virtue. "There is nothing more valuable and nothing more useful to ourselves" than virtue itself. Hence it is absurd to seek virtue for the sake of something else. To degrade it to the level of a means of attaining a reward or to induce it by threats destroys its value. Both attitudes are false. "God does not give men laws in order to reward them and to punish them." Thus those who expect God to reward them for their good actions "as though for the completest servitude" are far from the true idea and reality of virtue. They behave "as if virtue itself and the service of God were not happiness itself and the highest freedom."

Freedom from purpose is the principle of ethics; like the definition of God as *causa sui,* it involves a vicious circle.

Activity and serenity: Spinoza teaches the potential wise man to live entirely with God and entirely in the world. "A free man thinks of nothing less than of death, and his wisdom is not a meditation upon death but upon life." His conduct is not determined by fear of death; rather, he desires to do good, to live, and to preserve his being.

Spinoza bids the wise man to look upon all things, all events, and himself as necessary and invariable in their eternal essence and to find peace in this necessity, to participate in modal existence, recognizing its manifest necessity, to observe it and be above it. In Spinoza (as elsewhere throughout history) the idea of absolute necessity is a spur to activity; I am active because I know that I am doing what is necessary. The great difference between Spinoza and other believers in necessity (Calvin or Marx, for example) lies in their view of what is necessary.

Thus the intuition of necessity results in activity, but also in serenity: evil, folly, failure, the experience of my own ruin, all are necessary; consequently I do not revile my enemy, or the treacherous man, or the blind fool. There is no room for hatred or contempt. Rational insight finds necessity in all things. Value-free knowledge in the world, as far as such knowledge goes, gains an intimation of necessity, which is fully known by metaphysical consciousness. Even when it becomes necessary to differentiate, evaluate, and choose in human existence, this act of the mode does not conflict with the value-free attitude, for evaluation itself is seen as a factor in perfect necessity. Value-free knowledge operates in the conduct of rational beings: in extinguishing resentment, anger, and violence, in patience and watchful waiting, in the recognition of necessity in all its forms, even in the form of an alien, irrational existence.

Equanimity: Human strength is limited and is infinitely exceeded by the power of external causes. "We are disturbed by external causes in a number of ways, and like the waves of the sea agitated by contrary winds, we fluctuate in our ignorance of our future and destiny."

This state of the mode is unalterable. But philosophy "teaches us how we ought to behave with regard to the things of fortune, or those which are not in our power . . . for it teaches us with equal mind to wait for and bear each form of fortune." The striving of philosophy is "to make us more independent of hope, to free us from fear, [so that we may] command our fate to the best of our powers."

This we shall do if we regulate our actions and our thoughts and our imaginations "according to the clear counsel of reason." We shall meet contrary fortune with equanimity if we are aware that we have done our best and that our strength was not sufficient to enable us to avoid misfortune.

It is essential that we should be wholly permeated by the knowledge "that all things follow from the eternal decree of God, according to that same necessity by which it follows from the essence of a triangle that its three angles are equal to two right angles." Insight demands only what is necessary. Consequently, the striving "of the better part of our self" is consonant with the order of nature as a whole. For "whatever a man, who is after all a part of nature, does for his own sake, for his self-preservation, or what nature does to him without his participation, all this is effected only by the divine power which operates in part through his human nature and in part through external things." The highest happiness resides in harmony with divine necessity. But for Spinoza absolute necessity is God's being, substance, not the idea of some natural or historical process.

Insight into this necessity makes for fortitude, that is, the inspiring, powerful, active affects. Fortitude, for Spinoza, consists of strength of mind (*animositas*), which enables a man to live according to the decrees of reason, and generosity, which causes him, in sole obedience to the decree of reason, to help his fellow men and join with them in friendship.

The man of fortitude hates and envies no one, is angry with no one, underestimates no one, and is free from pride. He knows "that everything he conceives to be good and bad, and everything which appears to be disorderly, horrible, unjust, and shameful, springs from his disordered, perverted, and confused view of things." This confusion vanishes once he has understood the necessity of things. Then, indeed, "he will find nothing deserving of hatred, mockery, or contempt, nor will he pity anyone; rather, he will endeavor, to the best of his ability, to act well and be happy."

4. Characterization

The fundamental attitude recommended by Spinoza is distinguished from Stoic equanimity, to which it might seem related, by Spinoza's conception of God, which is different from the Stoic doctrine of God, just as Spinoza's third class of knowledge (*scientia intuitiva*) differs from Stoic reason, and as Spinoza's serene self-assertion differs from the Stoic assertion of a punctual, absolute self.

Spinoza lacks the violence of the Stoics. He does not teach men to drive or repress themselves. To his mind, such compulsion is ineffectual (an affect can only be combated by another affect) and fraught with disastrous and unnatural consequences. Reason does not combat an affect but lets it die away. Consequently, Spinoza's prescriptions are directed solely toward the efficacy of knowledge. Herein he knows himself to be cooperating with natural necessity. In Spinoza there is no torment, no defiance, no coercion. Beyond good and evil, he serenely accepts all things.

Nor can Spinoza's thinking be equated with the ethical demand of reason in Kant. Spinoza denies that any absolute demand springs from reason itself. Consequently he knows rules of life but no absolute imperatives, no prohibitions, no obedience to the recognized ethical law, nor the self-violation it implies. Where reason is kindled, the ethical life develops of itself, according to natural law, because natural law is divine and hence identical with reason.

Spinoza's understanding of Christ is characteristic of his philosophy. He held that Christ possessed such perfection as no other man. "No one except Christ received the revelations of God without the aid of imagination, whether in words or vision."

What Christ experienced, He translated into words, in large part adapted to the comprehension of the multitude. He "was not so much a prophet as a mouthpiece of God." He "perceived truly what was revealed . . . for a matter is understood when it is perceived by the mind without words or symbols." However, "He doubtless taught His doctrines as eternal truths and did not lay them down as laws." Spinoza was obviously thinking of Christ when he wrote: "It may be that God imprinted His idea so strongly on one man that for love of God that man would forget the world and would love other men as himself."

It has been thought that Spinoza contradicted his own philosophy in speaking of Christ in this way. Not at all. In the same context he says repeatedly that he does not understand the Church doctrine of Christ as son of God. And he goes on to say that if God is represented as a lawgiver or ruler and called just, compassionate, etc., this is "according to the people's power of understanding." In truth, says Spinoza, God acts purely from out of the necessity of His nature and perfection. "His decrees and volitions are eternal truths, and always involve necessity."

It is perfectly obvious that Spinoza sometimes, unavoidably and intentionally, adapts himself to the "people's capacity for understanding," especially in speaking of political matters. But this veneration of Christ is not such an adaptation. The certainty of God, which for Spinosa had precedence over all else, the love of God and man that filled him—all these he found in Jesus *the man*. Though he rarely said so, he revered Jesus above all other men, and the words in which he expressed this veneration suggest an identification of Jesus' knowledge of God, which he experienced directly from mind to mind, with Spinoza's own philosophical knowledge of God.

Although the path that Spinoza points out is difficult, it can assuredly be found. As he writes at the end of the *Ethics:* "It must indeed be difficult, since it is so seldom discovered; for if salvation lay ready at hand and could be discovered without great labor, how could it be possible that it should be neglected by almost everybody? But all noble things are as difficult as they are rare."

VIII. RELIGION AND THE STATE

Political thinking was at work in Spinoza's earliest, lost treatise. In it he protested against the anathema as it affected his civic existence. Political thinking remained with him for the rest of his life; it supplies the content of the longest and most powerful of the works that he himself published, the *Theologico-Political Treatise*, and of his last, unfinished work, the *Political Treatise*.

Man finds within himself two laws: the law arising from his bond with God and that arising from his bond with other men. The first bond is absolutely necessary, not so the second. For the law according to which a man lives before God and with God must be borne constantly in mind; whereas the law which springs from his bond with other men in the world of modes "is not so necessary, inasmuch as he can isolate himself from men." All his life Spinoza remembered these two laws, though he dropped the idea (expressed in his youth) that an individual can cut himself off from other men. He came to recognize that "*for man nothing is more useful than man.*" We can never arrive at the point where we require nothing from other men for the preservation of our existence. Our intelligence would be less complete if the mind knew nothing but itself. Without mutual aid men can neither live their lives nor develop their minds.

But despite this unique value of man for man, a reliable common bond is not achieved simply by free association among men. With all their similarity, men differ from one another. The same thing seems good to one and bad to another; to the one ordered, to the other confused; to the one pleasant, to another unpleasant. Hence such sayings as "Many men, many minds"; "Each man to his taste," and so on. This only goes to show that men would rather imagine things (according to the disposition of their minds) than know them (according to reason). Imaginations separate men, only reason brings them together. From the affections of the imagination spring disputes and ultimately skepticism; from reason spring harmony and true insight.

Consequently, the great impulse to agree with others is ambivalent. In the realm of the imagination it has an opposite effect: "Each man strives to the best of his ability to bring it about that others should love what he loves and hate what he hates. But inasmuch as all strive equally to this end, they impede one another equally; and inasmuch as all wish to be praised and loved by all, the outcome is mutual hatred." But in the realm of reason, the impulse attains its goal. It fulfills itself in the community by causing the one common truth to be revealed to all. There is nothing more desirable and "more precious for the preservation of (men's) being than that all should agree with all in such a way that all seem to form a single mind and a single body." Men who are guided by reason "seek nothing for themselves that they do not also desire for other men."

But such rules are not a sufficient foundation for real community. For men's life together is seldom determined by reason, but more often by the affective nature of men who do everything in accordance with their desires. Since rational men are extremely rare, a rational man understands that the state is indispensable to all men, to the rational as well as the irrational and antirational. For the state alone possesses a power that can check the power and arbitrary will of individuals.

The advantage of an ordered political community is far greater than the disadvantage. "Let satirists scoff at human affairs, let theologians denounce them, and let the melancholy praise a life rude and without refinement, despising men and admiring brutes, men will nevertheless find out . . . that it is only by their united strength that they can avoid the dangers which everywhere threaten them." To give up the state would be as absurd as the action of the young man who, after a scolding from his parents, leaves home and joins the army, preferring tyrannical discipline to domestic discomforts and the admonitions of his parents. The rational attitude is to accept offenses at the hands of men and the state with equanimity and zealously do what fosters harmony and friendship. "A man who is guided by reason is freer in a State where he lives according to the common laws than he is in solitude, where he obeys himself alone."

Toward the state as toward our destiny, Spinoza seems to demand a contradictory attitude: on the one hand, we should *recognize its necessity* and bear this necessity without fear; but on the other hand, we should conceive models and ideas of the best possible state, hence of the state that will prove best in our concrete situation, and act in accordance with it. Accordingly, Spinoza says that his philosophy is "of no little benefit to the political community, insofar as it teaches in what way the citizens are to be governed and guided, namely, in such a way that they should not serve as slaves, but should voluntarily do what is best." To the necessity of known events (events in the world of modes) he opposes the freedom of the active man, but both are included in all-encompassing divine necessity.

Thus this philosophy aspires to bring reason into political life by recognizing the nature of events in the world of modes, and arriving, on the basis of this knowledge, at norms according to which it is reasonable to act in making laws and shaping institutions.

Here a distinction must be made. In political life as in the life of the individual, the ultimate goal is clear: that as many men as possible should be philosophers, living in the perfection of reason based on the knowledge of God. But the norms are ambivalent. For in the ever-changing life of states there are several forms offering relative permanence; and here, as in the study of nature, no particular form can exhaust the infinite possibilities. There are several models, hence their virtue is relative, and in practice none can attain perfection. There is more than one path to betterment. The states and institutions that can be arrived at along these paths should be judged by ideal types set up in accordance with the criteria of such inherent necessities as permanence, security, and freedom (Spinoza attempted to do this in his last political treatise).

Spinoza starts out by examining the requirements of political life independently, but after his initial exposition, religion occupies a central position in his discussion of the state. Hence the title of his most important work: *Theologico-Political Treatise.*

Here again we find an apparent contradiction, namely, between Spinoza's purely philosophical thinking and his theologico-political thinking. For when in a political context he discusses the origins of religious authority, in particular of the Bible, it is clear that he is not speaking in the area of the philosophical metaphysics of eternal necessity, but in that of human social existence, that is, in the world of the endless modes, with special reference to the situation in contemporary Holland. Moving in a different realm of knowledge, he seems—but only seems—to forget his philosophy when he sets forth political necessities and approaches religion itself as a politically active citizen.

A. Spinoza's Political Thinking

The reality of the state must be known through experience and not through the pure concept. For existence does not follow from the concept of essence (except in the case of God); the reality and subsistence of things are manifested only to experience. Consequently "statesmen have written much more aptly about politics than have philosophers." Because they had experience, they taught "what is consonant with practice." Spinoza held Machiavelli in high esteem. He himself aspired to supply nothing new, but "only to represent in a sure and incontrovertible way what is most compatible with practice."

His starting point, in the *Political Treatise*, is the observation of human nature: In their overwhelming majority, men are guided not by reason, but by passions. Every man would like others to live according to his opinion; consequently, men come into conflict and do their utmost to oppress one another. They pity the unfortunate and envy the fortunate, but incline more to vengeance than to compassion. "Although all are persuaded that religion teaches every man to love his neighbor as himself . . . yet this persuasion has little power over the passions." It asserts itself on the deathbed, when sickness has quelled the passions and a man lies helpless, or in church, "where men do not deal with one another, but not at all . . . in the law-court or the palace." Reason, to be sure, can do a good deal to moderate the affects, but its path is always an arduous one. It is as wonderful as it is rare. Hence it is pure fantasy to suppose "that the multitude of men distracted by politics can ever be induced to live according to the bare dictate of reason."

Experience further teaches that men are exceedingly different. Some peoples are barbarous and servile (the Turks), others are freedom-loving (the Dutch).

A. PRINCIPLES OF NECESSITY IN POLITICAL LIFE

1. *Spinoza's principles of natural right*

a. Everything that is, including man, desires to persist in being, and consequently to assert itself against dangers and obstacles. What is and asserts itself has might. Its might is its right.

b. Spinoza calls the principle according to which power increases and decreases *natural right.* In common usage, natural right designates a body of norms which are valid for men in every condition, even when they are not followed. But Spinoza has in mind the reality of actual events. Disregarding such ideal norms, Spinoza says: The more might, the more right; where there is no might, there is also no right. Natural might is itself the law of necessity. Right is not something that should be, but something that is. "By natural right I understand the very laws or rules of nature, in accordance with which everything takes place. . . . And so the natural right . . . of every individual thing extends as far as its power; and accordingly, whatever any man does after the laws of his nature, he does by the highest natural right."

c. *Reason* as such is the greatest might. Its weakness is that it is so rare among men. But it is not entirely powerless. Statesmanship treats both reason and the passions as factors, the latter being so much more powerful only because in practice they are so much more widespread. Both are natural. In this connection no distinction is recognized "between desires springing from reason and those springing from other sources."

"If human nature had been so constituted that man should live according to the mere dictate of reason . . . in that case natural right, considered as special to mankind, would be determined by the power of reason only. But men are more led by blind desire than by reason: and therefore the natural power or right of human beings should be limited not by reason, but by every appetite whereby they are determined to action."

d. *The origin of the state* should be understood on the basis of natural right, not of a rational plan. Because all men create some sort of political institutions, "we must not try to derive the causes and natural foundations of the state from doctrines of reason, but must take them from the universal nature and disposition of man." Men are by nature enemies in envy, anger, and hatred. My worst enemy is the man I most fear. A man strives in vain to defend himself singly against all. Hence the natural right of the individual, because it is determined by his might, is virtually nonexistent. The more ground for fear he has, the less might he has and the less right. But the more men band together, the more might and hence right they acquire.

From this it follows that we can properly speak of natural right as a characteristic of man only where men in common have rights, where they secure the land they inhabit and cultivate against all violence and live according to the common will of the community. In such countries all may be said to live according to one mind.

e. In this *political condition* the individual has "only as much right to nature as the common law accords him." He is subject "to the concerted will of the community charged with care for the commonwealth," namely the right to make, interpret, and repeal laws, to decide on questions of war and peace. This government can be a democracy (government by an assembly constituted by the whole people) or an aristocracy (government by a few privileged persons) or a monarchy (government by one man).

f. It is only through the state that there exist *laws,* which are not necessarily compelling laws of nature, but civil laws which demand but do not always obtain obedience. "Wrongdoing is conceivable only in a commonwealth, where the common law of the whole state decides what is good and what is evil. Obedience is the constant will to do what is good according to the law and what must be done in accordance with the decision of the community."

Only through the state do there exist *contracts,* which are enforced by the state's instruments of power. But what comes into being through the state is not the foundation or binding power of the state. What compels the citizen does not compel the state itself. Hence the treaties and agreements between states "remain valid so long as the will of him who gave his word remains unchanged. For he who has authority to break faith has, in fact, relinquished nothing of his own right, but only made a present of words. If then he, being by natural right judge in his own case, comes to the conclusion that more harm than profit will come of his promise, by the judgment of his own mind he decides that the promise should be broken, and by natural right he will break the same." (One who orders his life according to the rules of reason acts differently; even when no power compels him, he keeps his promise.) The state is compelled for its own sake to inspire fear and respect. However, the rules for doing so do not pertain to the domain of civil law, but to that of natural right. Fear and respect are maintained only through the right of war. "In order to remain free, a commonwealth must order its conduct according to no one but itself, and consider as good and bad nothing other than what it recognizes in its own mind as good and bad."

In accordance with natural right, the same independence toward laws and contracts applies in the relation of a state to its citizens. The state is not bound by what binds all its citizens. "Contracts or laws, by which the populace transfers its rights to a council or an individual man, must be broken as soon as the common good demands it."

But who decides what the common good requires? "No private citizen is entitled to judge." Only the possessor of state power is free to interpret the laws, which are not in fact binding upon him.

2. *The political process*

Does natural right permit the arbitrary use of power? It neither allows nor forbids, but lets the consequences of every action take effect. Breach of law and contract is permitted in accordance with the same natural right which causes mistaken action to result in the destruction of the state or the diminution of its power. A "criminal" may achieve lasting success by breach of law and contract; in this case, he is right according to natural right. Or he may be ruined by so doing, and then he is wrong. A commonwealth is subject to no other rules than man in the state of nature. But above all it must "not be its own enemy." Destruction of power is the punishment of natural right for arbitrary abuse of power. Breach of law and contract by a state diminishes the power of that state by transforming the common fear of most citizens into rebellion. "In such cases the state disintegrates. Accordingly, the possessor of government power is obliged to observe the conditions of a contract by the same motive which prevents a man in the state of nature from bringing about his own death." The equivalence of might and right means that an action which results in a lessening of power also leads to the loss of right. "A commonwealth then does wrong when it does, or suffers to be done, things which may be the cause of its own ruin; and we can say that it then does wrong in the sense in which philosophers or doctors say that nature does wrong; and in this sense we can say that a commonwealth does wrong when it acts against the dictates of reason."

For because the hallmark of power is permanence and stability, the power of the moment can be deceptive. Only a state guided by reason has permanence. Only reason results in permanence; the passions result in change. How does reason make itself felt in the state? Men are not rational, nor is the state as such. It is fear that first paves the way for reason. Thus motivations rejected by philosophical reason help the state to become rational: humility, repentance, the veneration of prophets.

Reason demands peace. But it is the striving for the permanence and security of state power that first impels men to desire peace. "More permanent than all others is the commonwealth which can only protect what has been acquired but not desire foreign acquisitions, and which therefore strives in every way to avert war and exerts every effort to preserve peace."

In order that the state should become rational, it does not suffice that a ruler (like one of the good Roman Emperors) should govern according to reason. A state cannot achieve permanence by being rationally and conscientiously governed by *one* man, for it then becomes dependent on this one man. It must, if it is to endure, "be so ordered that those charged with administering it cannot, regardless of whether they obey reason or their affects, be put into a position to act badly or unconscientiously. The security of a commonwealth is not affected by the motives that make men adhere to sound government, provided the government is sound. For freedom of mind and strength of mind are private virtues. Security is the virtue of the state."

Reason of state is necessitated by the passion itself, by the passionate will of a ruler who desires the permanence and security of his own power. But reason as such is to be expected neither of the multitude nor of leading politicians. For both are driven by passions.

Fear alone holds them in check. Commenting on the dictum "Terrible is the crowd when it is not afraid," Spinoza says: To suppose that the populace is without moderation, that it serves slavishly or rules arrogantly, that it is terrible when it is not afraid, is to limit "all errors to the common people" and to forget that nature is the same in all. All men are arrogant when they rule and terrible when they are not afraid, and everywhere "truth is most falsified by the embittered and by servile minds."

Thus it is the passion for secure power that necessitates the realization of reason in the state. This is a necessary consequence of the enduring tension in political life. Every individual, to be sure, has made over to the state the right "to live as he pleases," at the same time entrusting the state with "the power to defend him." But "no one can be robbed of the right to defend himself to such a degree that he ceases to be a man." Consequently, "the subjects have retained, by natural right as it were, what cannot be taken from them without great danger to the state." Just as the anarchic self-will of the individual leads the state to intervene against him, so the arbitrary power of the rulers leads to the rebellion of the people.

The state does not exist through reason alone; the concept of a state does not suffice to bring one into existence. "The coming-into-existence and survival of natural things cannot be deduced from their definition. For their conceptual essence remains the same." But what has power as its origin requires power for its survival. "In order to endure, things require the same power as they needed in order to enter into existence."

Spinoza's political thinking encounters an antinomy. On the one hand, the natural foundations of the state "cannot be derived from the principles of reason but must be taken from the universal nature of men." And on the other, a stable state endures solely through reason, which, to be sure, is not its foundation, but is necessitated by the ruling power's need for security and permanence.

3. Encompassing necessity

We may speak of natural right but not of natural wrong. Everything has right insofar as it has might. Wrongdoing, injustice, presupposes the existence of the state as a law-giving power. But all this right and wrong are encompassed in the right of necessity.

Though laws may be given by states and proclaimed by prophets, they all exist through the power of God. But God's right, the power that encompasses all others, is superordinate to every particular law and to every legal order. When we obey the laws of the state and the laws of God as proclaimed by the Prophets, we must never forget "that we are in God's power as clay in the power of the potter." "Man, to be sure, can act in opposition to God's decrees, as they are inscribed like laws in our minds or the minds of the Prophets, but never to the eternal decision of God, which is inscribed in all nature and governs the order of all nature."

This distinction must be understood if we are not to miss the philosophical meaning of all Spinoza's political thinking. What does Spinoza mean by "all nature"? He means *natura naturata* in its totality, upon which God, or *natura naturans* (hence *deus sive natura*), inscribes a law that encompasses and transcends all particular laws.

The laws of nature are disclosed in *natura naturata,* the cosmos. Just as Spinoza endows God with infinitely many attributes, so he imputes infinitely many laws to *natura naturata.* Our knowledge of these laws is for all time "fragmentary, because the order and system of all nature remains largely unknown to us." Are then, we ask, the eternally necessary laws of nature identical with the laws that are knowable, and in part known to us, through the natural sciences? Spinoza answers in the affirmative. But can all cosmic reality, nature as *natura naturata,* be encompassed in a system of natural laws? Only by God's infinite intellect, says Spinoza, not by us. For neither by experience nor by its concepts can our finite understanding know the infinite reality of the cosmos, though it is well able to arrive at an adequate theoretical conception of infinity itself. For Spinoza the magnitude of all-encompassing nature is infinitely more than known nature and than our reason, which is effective in the knowledge of finite things. To our finite reason, much in nature "seems ridiculous, absurd, or evil.". But "in fact, what our reason pronounces bad is not bad as regards the order and laws of universal nature, but only as regards the laws of our own nature taken separately," because we "should like to see everything directed according to the rule of our reason." Nature "is not subject to the laws of human reason, which aim only at the true profit and preservation of man; but to innumerable other laws, which relate to the eternal order of universal nature."

The finite laws of nature, which are known to us, relate to something that is inferior to philosophical reason and freedom. But the encompassing divine law of eternal necessity is above everything we can definitely know. It encompasses and transcends all finite knowledge and its utilization as a means to ends as well as every law that is given in the form of ethical obligation in society.

Spinoza elucidates this fundamental situation in detail. "Man, whether a wise man or a fool, is a part of nature." Reason and desire are equally subordinate to nature. "Whether governed by reason or by mere desire, man always acts in accordance with the laws and rules of nature, that is, according to natural right."

It is a mistake to suppose that fools do not follow but only confuse the order of nature. Most particularly it is an error to suppose that the human mind was created directly by God, that man in nature resembles a state within the state, wholly independent of other things, possessing absolute power to determine his own destiny and to make proper use of his reason. Experience teaches the contrary. It is no more in our power to have a sound mind than a sound body. And it is not within our power to determine whether we shall live by reason or follow blind desire.

The theologians say that this weakness of mankind derives from the original sin of Adam. But if the first man was incorrupt and had power over his mind, how could he fall? Because he was deceived by the Devil, the theologians reply. But who deceived the Devil? Who was able to instill such madness in the first of all rational creatures that he desired to be more than God? Surely not this creature himself. How could the first man, if he was master of his mind and lord of his will, allow himself to be seduced and his mind to be confused? Accordingly, it must be "admitted that it was not in the first man's power to make proper use of his reason; he was just as subject to the passions as we are."

To sum up this view, fundamental to Spinoza, of the all-embracing necessity of God, or nature: According to the finite and limited judgment of his own understanding, man is subject to what is for him the most terrible of evils, namely, total annihilation. But he is not caught up in a chaos of blind natural forces. For even if he should fall from all humanly sheltered and sheltering existence, he cannot fall away from the world and from God. He is always in the hand of God, because he partakes of eternal necessity, from which he cannot escape and in which he finds himself. By philosophical insight he knows that he and everything that befalls him are part of eternal necessity. This knowledge appeases his spirit and gives him peace. Spinoza does not complain, he does not find fault with things as they are. In him there is nothing of a Job. But his serenity is not the indifference of an irrationalist or amoralist; it springs from the love of God.

B. THE IDEAL STATE

Spinoza's account of the affects as necessary forces is followed by a picture of the philosopher in the freedom of his reason. His exposition of the natural theory of the state is followed by a picture of the right state.

The coolness with which Spinoza discusses the practical necessities of political life gives way to a restrained enthusiasm when he speaks of reason and freedom in the state. Amid the opaque necessity of the finite things of nature, a philosopher who thinks politically and pursues political aims turns to reason. For reason is itself a factor in the all-embracing necessity of nature. The natural striving of reason for self-realization is also a part of nature. In the state, it aspires to attain the best possible condition of the human community, in which all individuals will be enabled to live and to think in freedom, thanks to a legality recognized by common consent. Where there is reason there is harmony, and only where reason prevails can all the truly human potentialities be realized. Accordingly, Spinoza finds in man "not merely the circulation of the blood, but first and foremost what is termed reason, true *virtus,* and the true life of the mind."

1. *Freedom:* Spinoza elucidates the nature of political freedom:

I have another man in my power if I have (1) bound him, (2) deprived him of his weapons and of the means to defend himself or run away, (3) inspired him with fear, or (4) so obligated him with rewards that he would rather obey me than himself and rather live as I see fit than as he himself sees fit. In the first and second cases, the wielder of power possesses only the body of the man he has deprived of his freedom, but not his mind; in the third and fourth, he has subjected the mind as well as the body, but only as long as fear or hope is maintained.

But even when deprived of his freedom, every individual remains under his own right, which has only seemingly been destroyed. As soon as he ceases to fear violence and hope for reward, this right recovers its effectiveness. A man remains under his own right by virtue of his mind, which belongs to him as a man. But even his mind is under its own right only insofar as it can make proper use of reason. "Judgment can also become subject to alien right insofar as one mind can be deceived by another."

The purpose of political freedom is to make room for the freedom of reason. Man's reason as such is his freedom and greatest power. "Nay, inasmuch as human power is to be reckoned less by physical vigor than by mental strength, it follows that those men are most independent whose reason is strongest, and who are most guided by it. And so I am altogether for calling a man so far free as he is led by reason."

Man is the more free, the more he is at one with himself, the more he loves God. Hence "reason teaches us to practice piety and to be of good and tranquil mind." But this is possible only in the state.

2. *Stability and freedom:* In the natural theory of the state the criterion of the good state was stability. But the goal of the ideal state is freedom. This primacy of freedom throws a new light on the criterion of stability, for the essential now is not stability as such but freedom in stability. Mere stability can be deceptive. Where political freedom is at stake, Spinoza, who does not wish "to condemn, lament, despise, or deplore," hands down radical judgments. In this connection his love of peace, which elsewhere seems unconditional, is suspended. For a state can have stability without freedom. Turkey is an example. "A commonwealth whose peaceful condition depends on the cowardice of its subjects, who let themselves be led like cattle and learn only to serve, can more aptly be called a wilderness than a state." "Peace is not freedom from war but a virtue, which springs from strength of mind." "If

slavery, barbarism, and desolation are called peace, then there is nothing more pitiful for man than peace. For peace does not consist in the absence of war but in a unity and harmony of minds."

Spinoza once drew a picture of himself dressed as Masaniello, the then famous Neapolitan revolutionary. This peace-loving, reasonable man, who desired nothing more than harmony with his fellow men and peace in God, knew that where rational, political freedom was at stake he had the strength of a rebel within him.

Spinoza discusses publicity, because he regards it as essential to political freedom. Only a ruler intent on absolute domination maintains that the interest of the state requires his affairs to be carried on in secret. He praises Machiavelli, who "was for freedom and gave the most salutary counsels for its defense." This "very astute man" showed "how unintelligently many persons act, who try to do away with a tyrant when they have been unable to do away with the causes that make a prince into a tyrant." But above all Machiavelli wished to show "how very careful a free people must be not to entrust its welfare unreservedly to one man." Spinoza attaches little importance to the question of whether monarchy, aristocracy, or democracy is the best form of government. The all-important question is to establish, within each of the three forms, the best possible type from the standpoint of stability and freedom.

3. *For whom did Spinoza write?* For whose benefit did Spinoza divulge his ideas? By whom did he wish to be read? He said: "I know that it is impossible to rid the people of superstition and fear. I know that the perseverance of the people is obstinacy, and that they are not guided by reason but carried away by blind passion for better or worse. Consequently, I do not invite the people or any of those who share the same affects to read this." Despite its relevance to the political situation of Holland, the *Theologico-Political Treatise* is written not in Dutch but in Latin. Spinoza addressed himself to the educated man who was prepared for reason and possessed a true yearning for freedom. His aim was to raise to full consciousness what such readers already desired.

SPINOZA AND HOBBES

Spinoza had great praise for Machiavelli but borrowed few ideas from him. He scarcely mentions Hobbes, with whom many of his own ideas clearly originated. The only plausible explanation is that Spinoza felt a kinship of mind with Machiavelli and not with Hobbes. Purely rational ideas are as such a means of communication; in their universality they are mere forms, to which no right of possession can be acquired. It is worth-while to examine the difference between Spinoza and Hobbes.

For Hobbes the ultimate motive of political life is security against violent death; for Spinoza it is freedom. Thus in Spinoza all the elements taken from Hobbes acquire a new meaning:

For both, the purpose of the state is the preservation of life. But for Spinoza this is not the ultimate end. To his mind, government loses its meaning when men cease to be rational beings and become subjects obeying out of fear. For the ultimate end of the state is not security but freedom, in which men can develop the powers of their body and mind and attain to reason.

Hobbes' reason constructs and calculates the conditions of security, one of which is absolute rule. Spinoza's reason is the knowledge of God and the love of man. Thus in the medium of a natural theory of the state, which largely coincides with Hobbes, Spinoza develops aims that are alien to Hobbes. Hobbes' reason is calculating and utilitarian, interested primarily in securing the peace. Spinoza's reason, which is his first and all-embracing concern, is an intuition and certainty of God.

Hobbes does not deal with religion, except to say that if peace and security are to be guaranteed, all questions of cult and dogma must be decided exclusively by the state. Spinoza is in the religious tradition, whose true content he develops as philosophical reason. Hobbes looks upon religion as largely superfluous. Spinoza recognizes its necessity for the multitude who lack insight and are incapable of philosophical reason.

Hobbes looks upon all men as equal: every man is capable of killing another; all have the same faculty of thought; through proper methods of thought, every man can become the equal of every other; there are no natural differences among men. For security in the state it suffices to elaborate a proper apparatus of institutions and laws. Spinoza concedes that because most men are incapable of philosophy, they require something which is not philosophy but religion, and which differs from vulgar superstition only in that it is recognized by the state or establishes an order which is the foundation of the state ("On the State of the Hebrews," in the *Theologico-Political Treatise*). Since the people are many and philosophers are but few, the reason of the state must be based on the attributes of the multitude.

Unlike Hobbes, Spinoza believes that some peoples more than others are endowed with a natural love of freedom. According to Spinoza, the good state derives its strength from this love of freedom. For this reason, he regards war as inevitable and holds that in war freedom will prove the stronger. "The supreme reward for armed service is freedom." Even in the state of nature, "each man expects no other reward from his warlike virtue than to be master of himself." "In war there can be no stronger or more powerful claim to victory than the image of freedom." "Assuredly those men fight most bravely who fight for home and hearth." No army of mercenaries can resist an army that is fighting for freedom. Princes "can oppress the people by means of an army to whom they pay wages." But they must fear nothing so much "as a free army of the people, which has created the glory of its fatherland by its courage, its effort, and its blood."

Hobbes condemns all breach of contract, because its consequences are harmful under all circumstances. Spinoza recognizes it as a necessity which is in keeping with natural right, whether embodied in the will of the rulers concerned with the welfare of the state or in the rebellion of the people—and this necessity can be judged only by its consequences, according as they tend to preserve, save, or destroy the state. He recognizes, however, that a philosopher, living by the ethos of reason, is not prepared to break any treaty.

Hobbes sees progress in the technical mastery of nature and looks into the future with amazing optimism. Spinoza regards man's mastery over nature as a significant task, but for him it does not assume central importance. In his vision, the future is overshadowed by the present task (in Holland), and by eternal necessity, which knows no history.

B. Religion in the State

Spinoza speaks in the *Theologico-Political Treatise* of the piety which is indispensable to political freedom and which philosophically resides in reason, or certainty of God. It assumes reality for the common people as religion, or "obedience to God." We men, whether philosophers or believers in revelation, are obedient, but in two different ways. For God either revealed the commandments of reason as speaking within ourselves (in this case philosophical reason is powerful in its own right and spontaneously obedient to God), or He revealed them to the Prophets in the form of laws (and then they operate through the demand for blind obedience).

Since antiquity the political importance of religion—its value as a force for order and its power to impose order upon the people—has been discussed. There were two fundamental views. According to one, religion is an instrument of political domination. Critias declared religion to be an invention of wise statesmen, a means of guiding the multitude, which cannot be controlled by external power alone. In this view, it is a benevolent deception or simply an instrument of power, which through religion penetrates to the innermost souls of men. In the opposing view, religion is fundamental and enduring truth, common to all men. But there are degrees in the form of truth. In revelation, something is given which is adapted by reason. The degree of such rational penetration marks the level of philosophy. This was the view of Averroës, Maimonides, and Hegel.

Spinoza's position is neither of these. He looks upon religion as necessary for the people. Yet he himself does not partake of it. He stands aloof, but he does not reject it; he regards as necessary what he neither needs for himself nor views with sympathy: where there is reason, phantasms disappear. Reason does freely and reliably what religious obedience does un-freely and—because of the tendency to sectarianism inherent in all super-stition—unreliably.

Spinoza quotes Quintus Curtius Rufus, the Roman biographer of Alex-ander the Great: "Nothing controls the crowd more effectively than superstition." He recognizes the all-dominating reality of revealed faith in Judaism, Christianity, Islam. But is this superstition? Yes, says Spinoza. But he also says that, on the basis of this revelation, love and justice are demanded and through obedience partly obtained. Thus in practice this belief accords with reason, though it lacks the theoretical knowledge of reason. Spinoza therefore does not simply criticize revealed religion out of existence, he recognizes its rational core and declares it to be indispensable to the building of a free society.

The evil of superstition is the fanatical hatred of multiple superstitions for one another. This feature is especially marked in revealed religion despite its rational core; it is the dangerous, malignant aspect of revealed religion. In Spinoza's view, the only way of countering this danger politically is to deprive the church and its priests of all influence on the state; further, theology and philosophy must be kept strictly separate. Theology teaches obedience to faith, philosophy teaches rational knowledge. Both are justified in their spheres. But where they come into conflict, the result is incurable disharmony, because there is no common ground for discussion. The truth of philosophy is based on the universal concepts (*notiones communes*) that are common to all men; the truth of theology, on Holy Scripture. The former are known through the natural light, the latter through supernatural revelation.

Spinoza's central theologico-political idea is based on the impotence of the wise. Philosophers are by nature the mightiest of men, but they are numerically so few that they can play no role in the state. Neither the masses of the people nor the statesmen are guided by reason. Spinoza is far from the Platonic idea of a philosopher-king.

The philosopher must therefore say: The better we observe and know the customs and conditions of men, the more wisely we shall be able to live among them and the better we shall be able to adapt our actions to their character. Consequently, insight into the conditions of peace and security should lead the state to recognize revealed religion. Political thinking should be limited to the aims of the state; from this standpoint, revealed faith and philosophy are judged according to their advantages and the dangers they involve.

But all this political thinking is transcended. The state is not the ultimate goal. Its existence is only the condition for the highest possible development of each man. For this he requires freedom. This freedom encompasses an aim which points beyond the state, and at the same time, it is the condition of the security and permanence of the state itself.

Spinoza's *philosophical* rejection of religious faith is unequivocal. There can be no revelation. Does God reveal Himself in spoken words or immediately, without making use of something else? "Certainly not in words, for then man would have had to know the meaning of the words before they were addressed to him." If God says: "I am the Lord thy God," man, in order to understand, must previously, without the words, have known who God is. Thus Spinoza says it is impossible that God should have revealed Himself to man by any outward sign. Only the intellect of man can know God, since the intellect can neither exist nor be conceived of without God. Nothing is so close to the intellect as God. In order to reveal Himself to man, God needs Himself alone, not words, miracles, inspirations, or any other created thing.

Yet because men, the rulers as well as the ruled, are as they are, neither revelation nor miracles are to be despised in the ordering of state affairs, and not only because these imaginings are ineradicable, but also because superstition can take on a form compatible with the truth of philosophy (which is realized through reason as knowledge of God, charity, affability, and harmony) and because superstition or religion thus prepares the way for rational truth. Thus piety can be achieved not only on the basis of philosophical independence, but also, and indeed for the majority, through obedience to the law, through faith in the revelation contained in sacred books.

Nevertheless, superstition, which is still with us in the form of religion, conceals great dangers for the commonweal. It drives men to fanatical exclusiveness and violence, because, unlike reason which thinks the one God, it is multiple. Only reason binds; superstition divides. Spinoza expresses his surprise "that men who boast of professing the Christian religion, that is, love, joy, peace, moderation, and loyalty to all, nevertheless quarrel most bitterly among themselves"—that "each one, whether Christian, Turk, Jew, or heathen, can be recognized only by his outward appearance and his cult; in other respects all have the same mode of life"—"that the people consider it part of religion to look upon Church offices as dignities and benefices and to hold the clergy in high honor."

This universal superstition gives rise to tyranny, which, where the means are available, restricts the freedom of each man to develop in accordance with his own nature, forbids free thought, and strives for control over the state.

In the face of this politico-theological reality, Spinoza devotes his thinking to the cause of freedom. "It is utterly contrary to universal freedom that every man's free judgment should be restricted by prejudices or curtailed in any way . . . that opinions should be considered punishable after the manner of crimes." This is why differences of opinion lead to disorder and rebellion. Such evils would be impossible if, in accordance with the law of the state, "only acts were judged, but words exempted from punishment." Spinoza sets out to show that freedom (of judgment, and freedom to worship God in one's own way) "can be permitted without danger to religion and the peace of the state, and moreover that to do away with it is to do away with religion and political peace."

A. REASON AND REVELATION

Catholics, Protestants, and Jews base their religion on revelation. The historical reality of faith and its importance for life in society led Spinoza to "evaluate Holy Writ or revelation very highly from the standpoint of its utility and necessity." For, "since all men are capable of unconditional obedience and only a very few attain to a virtuous way of life by the mere guidance of reason, we should have to doubt of the salvation of almost all men if we did not have the testimony of Scripture." It would be folly, "merely because it cannot be demonstrated by mathematics, not to recognize something which has been confirmed by the testimony of so many Prophets, which has brought so much consolation precisely to those who are not strong of mind, which has been of no little utility to the state, and which we can believe without harm or danger." If we are to order our lives wisely, we may not accept as true only that which there is no reason to doubt—"As though most of our actions were not highly uncertain and a prey to chance."

Yet from a philosophical standpoint Spinoza regards revelation as impossible. Such statements as the above are made only in a political context, and he recognizes revelation only in a particular sense. (1) He is able to describe and characterize revelation as one of the innumerable phenomena existing in the world of modes, but he cannot explain it except in relation to the needs of finite thinking beings. (2) In discussing these things, Spinoza knowingly speaks "according to the comprehension of the multitude," and here "multitude" includes the circle of enlightened men for whom he is writing this particular work. (3) Spinoza takes the point of view of the oligarchical party, where a liberal, tolerant faith was taken for granted.

But the essential point for Spinoza is that he finds the Biblical laws of love and righteousness to be in full agreement with the prescriptions of reason, and sees "the word of God," not in certain canonical writings, but only in these prescriptions. The Prophets, he declares, "taught no morality that is not in perfect agreement with reason. For it is no mere accident that the word of God in the Prophets agrees perfectly with the word of God that speaks within us."

But then Spinoza turns to the disastrous struggle of the denominations and their theologians against those whom they regard as heretics. By way of putting an end to such disputes, he regards a clear separation between reason and revelation as expedient and necessary. They are two different realms: "Reason is the realm of truth and wisdom, theology that of piety and obedience."

The truth of theology is restricted to the practice of obedience, namely, the practice of love and righteousness. Hence it should define the dogmas of faith only insofar as it is necessary for this obedience. "But it should leave the more precise definition of these dogmas to reason, which is the true light of the mind, without which the mind sees only dream figures and phantasms." Theological pseudo-knowledge is not only harmful, but also unnecessary for faith. "We know for certain that those things which without prejudice to love men can dispense with knowing, have no bearing on theology or on the word of God."

But the two realms are connected. For man is one and undivided. If he is obedient in faith and wise in reason, reason appears in faith insofar as faith thinks, and faith in reason, insofar as it becomes an object of reason.

But disastrous errors arise when the boundary between the two communicating realms is not kept clearly in mind. "Neither must theology be subservient to reason nor reason to theology; each must assert itself in its own sphere." Each "has its own realm, in which the other should not contradict it."

Since what is believed in obedience cannot be proved by reason, why, Spinoza asks, "do we believe in it?" If we accept it without reason like blind men, we are acting foolishly and without judgment. But if on the other hand we were to maintain that the foundation of obedience can be proved by reason, theology would be an inseparable part of philosophy. And Spinoza replies: "Without restriction I maintain that the fundamental dogma of theology cannot be explained by natural enlightenment, and that for this reason revelation was very necessary; nevertheless, we can make use of our judgment in order at least to recognize with moral certainty what has already been revealed. We must not expect to attain greater certainty concerning it than the Prophets themselves, whose certainty was only a moral one."

Their authority cannot be substantiated by mathematical proofs. It can be demonstrated by no other and no stronger arguments than those with which the Prophets in their time convinced the people, namely, first by a lively imagination, second by "signs," such as the occurrence of predicted events, third, by a good and righteous frame of mind. Consequently, even where the signs are confirmed, we owe the Prophets belief only when they recommend righteousness and love beyond all things, and teach them with an upright heart.

When contradictions arise between the tenets of philosophy and of theology, Spinoza denies that theology can justify its principles. At first, to be sure, he justifies the efforts of the theologians to build a solid foundation for theology, and to demonstrate it. "For who would wish to renounce truth or despise science and deny the certainty of reason?" But later on he finds them unforgivable. For in attempting to justify theology by reason, they are "asking the help of reason to banish reason." The theologians

seek "to justify authority by proofs, in order to rob reason and natural enlightenment of their authority." Or they pretend to submit theology to
the rule of reason, on "the supposition that the authority of theology has
radiance only when illumined by the natural light of reason."

But theology gains nothing by such attempts to overstep its limits and
become knowledge. In matters of insight, only reason can testify. Anyone
who invokes another witness speaks from the prejudice of his affects. "But
in vain, for what sort of altar can that man build who offends against the
majesty of reason?"

B. THE UNDERSTANDING OF THE BIBLE

Jews, Catholics, and Protestants base the claims of their faith on the Bible.
All argue with Bible quotations. The interpretation of the Bible is a power
not only for faith, but also for political ends. In order to avert the harm
done by this power in creating conflicts, often with bloody consequences,
Spinoza advocates the "right interpretation of the Bible."

Exegesis can be based on two fundamentally different assumptions. The
question arises: Are they mutually exclusive, or can they be reconciled?

The first assumption is that the Bible is the word of God. Being of
fundamentally different origin from all other books written by men, it
alone is Holy Scripture. Since it is the word of God, it can contain no
contradictions. Everything in it is true.

The second assumption is that the Bible is a collection of books written
by men, and originally no different in character from other works of literature.

Interpretation of the Bible according to the first assumption involves
the following methods:

1. If no contradiction is admissible in the Bible, the exegete must eliminate
the numerous contradictions that actually occur (as well as the objectionable
passages) by invoking an allegorical sense in addition to the literal sense.
2. The irrationality of the text is interpreted as a mystery. The exegete endeavors "to explain the absurdity" by supposing "the profoundest mysteries
to be concealed in the text." 3. An attempt is made to adapt Scripture to
reason, for example, to Aristotelian or Platonic speculations. Because Scripture is divine, hence true throughout, the exegete assumes that study of it
will disclose what philosophically he already knows.

Spinoza often attacks Maimonides, in whom he finds these false methods.
Maimonides assumes that the Prophets accord with one another and that
they were great philosophers and theologians, who concealed their ideas
in images addressed to the people, that the words of Scripture must be interpreted not according to their literal sense but in accordance with the pre-

conceived opinions of the exegetes, and that the meaning of Scripture cannot be gathered from Scripture itself.

These methods of exegesis contradict the pure evidence of unprejudiced reason. They rest on authority, that of the Pharisaic tradition, of the institutionally recognized scholars, of the Popes. The guarantor of truth becomes a reason grounded in authority, not the free reason which is its own foundation.

Spinoza rejects such methods on the strength of the other assumption: the Bible must be understood in a natural way, like any other book. He "undertook to examine Scripture afresh, with a free and unbiased mind." His methods are as follows:

1. His first principle is to make no assumption concerning the Bible which cannot be supported by the text, to impute no doctrine to it which is not clearly stated in the Bible itself. 2. To investigate how each individual book came into being, at what time and place, under what circumstances and in what situations, by whom and for whom it was written, and to consider the life, customs, and aspirations of the author. "The better we know a man's mind and way of thinking, the better able we shall be to interpret his words." 3. The history of all Prophetic books should be studied: through whose hands they passed, what variants of the text exist; who decided to include them among the Holy Scriptures, how they are organized into a whole. 4. To collate everything relating to the same subject, including what is ambiguous or seemingly contradictory. 5. The question of whether the meaning of a passage has been properly established must not be confused with the question of the truth of its content. Historical exegesis is concerned with the intended meaning, not with the truth of this meaning. We should determine the former, but make no decision as to the latter.

These methods led Spinoza to found modern Bible study as a branch of historical research. He recognized the importance of the Hebrew language: "Because all the authors of the Old and New Testament were Hebrews, a history of the Hebrew language is first of all indispensable." The books of the New Testament are to be sure couched in another language, "but they are Hebrew in character." The Bible as a whole is a product of the Jews. Every part of the Old and New Testaments was written by Jews. The question of whether a given element in the Bible is Jewish or Christian is of secondary importance to the historian.

But the question of truth is of burning interest to Spinoza. Hence he does not limit himself to ascertaining historical fact. He interprets, but on the basis of natural reason. He regards the Prophets as men endowed with heightened imagination, which for him diminishes truth. He further interprets this imaginative character in the Biblical texts by saying "that the teachings of Scripture are adapted to the intelligence and opinions of those to whom the Prophets and the Apostles preached the word of God, in order that men might accept it without resistance and with their whole hearts." In an extraordinary simplification of the Bible, he interprets the truth of its teachings: "I show that the revealed word of God does not reside in a given number of books, but in the simple concept of the divine spirit, as it was revealed to the Prophets: to obey God with one's whole soul, by practicing righteousness and love." Accordingly, Spinoza says that "the authority of the Prophets is meaningful only in questions of life conduct and true virtue, that in other matters their views are of little concern to us." In particular, he interprets the mass of Mosaic legislation (in contradistinction to the Ten Commandments, which are concerned with the right conduct of life): it was "solely the legal order of the Hebrew kingdom," which accordingly had no reason to be accepted by anyone but the Hebrews, and to which "they themselves were bound only so long as their state endured."

Spinoza interprets some of the contradictions in the Bible historically, by considering in what situation and for what reason a statement was made. The oldest books of the Bible breathe a warlike spirit. But Jesus said: "Whosoever shall smite thee on thy right cheek, turn to him the other also" (Matthew 5:17). Here He speaks not as a lawgiver (for He did not wish to destroy the law of Moses) but as a teacher of oppressed men in a corrupted state, whose destruction He held to be impending. In Lamentations, Jeremiah spoke similarly in a similar situation. But only in such times would Jesus and Jeremiah have bidden men to suffer injustice. In a good state, they would have said the exact opposite.

C. FREEDOM OF THOUGHT

Spinoza's interest in the understanding of the Bible had its source in the bloody conflicts over interpretation and in his rejection of all interpretations based on authority, regardless of where they originated.

Since men are different, said Spinoza in opposition to all authoritarian claims, each man must be granted freedom of judgment and the opportunity to develop the foundations of his faith as he sees fit. He justifies this thesis by the following arguments.

1. Whether a man is pious or godless should be judged solely by his works, not by his opinions and professions. "Only thus will all be enabled to obey God freely and only thus will righteousness and love come to be esteemed by all."

2. A distinction must be made between the true authority of the state, to which every citizen should bow, and the false authority of religious dogmas and laws. The law of the state relates, and rightly so, to outward actions; religion is concerned with an inner attitude, from which acts of love and righteousness follow freely, and not through coercion.

The laws of Moses were once state laws. They then rightly claimed public authority. "For if the individual had the right to interpret public law as he saw fit, no state could endure." The old Hebrew state is no more; our states are no longer theocracies. Religion today has relevance solely to "simplicity and trueness of heart," to love and righteousness. But "no one can be coerced into beatitude." Instead of force, "fraternal admonition" is in order, and "above all individual freedom of judgment is required." Thence it follows that in matters of religion each man is entitled to complete freedom of opinion. It is inconceivable that anyone should renounce this right. Just as the state is the supreme authority in interpreting the laws, because here public right is involved, so each individual is the supreme authority in explaining religion, because it falls under the right of the individual.

3. This free interpretation, implying also the science and criticism of the Bible, is possible only in a free state. "In a free state every man is allowed to think what he will and to say what he thinks." Spinoza argued this position with passion:

a) Freedom of thought is a part of the natural right of every individual, and cannot be alienated even to the natural right of the state. For according to the highest natural right, every man is master of his thoughts. Consequently "the supreme powers will never cause men to renounce the right to judge things as they see fit, in accordance sometimes with one and sometimes with another affect."

b) It is true that the supreme powers have the right to consider everyone as an enemy who does not in all his actions agree with them unconditionally. But government is tyranny if it extends to men's minds, that is, tries to prescribe what each mind should accept and what it should reject as false.

It is not any transcendent, eternal right of man that forbids a government to exercise such tyranny but the natural right of the state, for only in this way can it endure, avoid the evils of revolt and strife, and attain the goal of a free life for all. Thus Spinoza shows that freedom of thought redounds to the advantage of the state. Violence against the mind is a danger to the whole state and is incompatible with sound reason; it can only lead to the annihilation of the state.

c) The consequence of violence against the mind is that base men gain power. The anger of those who tolerate no free minds in their midst can easily transform the bigotry of a riotous populace into madness. Such men stir up the insolent mob against the authors of books that they consider undesirable. A state ruled by such men can tolerate no noble spirits. Men whose minds are free are declared to be enemies, banished, and threatened with death. But they do not fear death like criminals; they consider it an honor to die for freedom. Laws concerning opinion strike not the wicked but the noble.

Where such laws prevail, peace becomes impossible. Where the state authorities seek to settle quarrels among scholars by laws, conflicts arise, not through zeal for the truth but through lust for domination. The true breakers of the peace in a state are those who wish to destroy freedom of judgment, which cannot be repressed.

d) Freedom of thought must be distinguished from freedom of action. In respect to action Spinoza formulates the following fundamental situation: In a state, each man, pursuant to reason, decides once and for all to transfer his right to act according to his own judgment to the decision of the supreme power. To be sure, unanimous decisions are rare; "but every decision is looked upon as a decision of the whole community, of those who have voted against it as well as those who have voted for it." But since in human societies the decision of all can in practice be determined only through the majority, its application is limited. It is applicable only to actions and not to thoughts. Moreover, each decision is made with the reservation "that it will be modified if something better should appear." Those who are outvoted comply in their actions, not in their thoughts. Accordingly, a state must be so governed "that men whose opinions are openly at variance may nevertheless live in harmony."

But Spinoza sets limits to the free expression of opinion. Freedom of faith and freedom to philosophize remain unrestricted. But it should be determined what opinions in the state are "subversive" to the state order and the freedom of all, or, in other words, to what extent each man can be allowed the freedom to speak without prejudice to the peace of the state. Unrestricted freedom of thought and hence of speech is permitted each man only on condition "that he speak or teach simply and with the sole help of reason, but not put forward his opinion with deception, anger, and hatred." The restriction of affective speech is no less necessary than freedom of rational speech for the preservation of peace.

C. Critical Characterization of Spinoza's Views of Religion and Politics

A. LACK OF CLARITY AS TO THE RELATIONSHIP BETWEEN SCIENCE AND PHILOSOPHY

Science and philosophy were for Spinoza, as for all the thinkers of his time (and for many even today), the same. Spinoza spoke in the name of the one science, which through natural reason presupposes, and tries to find, one truth that is valid for all reason. But Spinoza is doing two very different things when on the one hand he employs the methods of science, interpreted as universally valid knowledge, to attack the assertions of the theologians or of the Bible, which can be proved to be historically or scientifically false, and when, on the other hand, in the name of reason (as philosophy), he declares other views of being or of ethical practice to be errors. In the first case, the power of universally valid knowledge is opposed to errors, and this power is indeed inescapable for every thinking man (when, for example, the miracle of Joshua, resurrection in the flesh, Moses' authorship of the Pentateuch are considered from the standpoint of astronomy, physics, biology, or history). In the second case faith stands against faith.

Confidence in universal agreement through the one reason is justified only in science. But this agreement does not apply to men in their whole being; it resides only in an everywhere identical, abstract area of understanding, which is removed from the richness of life or rather does away with it: men, for example, are agreed as to the rules governing the atomic process, but this does not prevent them from dropping atom bombs on each other's cities. It is a mistake to suppose that science brings men together. A very different matter is the reason which wholly permeates man's being, which is the medium of each man's irreplaceable existence, the reason which is dependent on unlimited openness to communication and is determined to achieve it. But this reason does not bring about *agreement* among men. It admits of an unlimited diversity of ways of life, of conceptions of Being and of God. In it the historically unique reality of each existence sees and questions itself and lets itself be questioned. This diversity cannot be combined in *one* man. But where there is reason, the drive to communication is unlimited, not only in order that each man may know the reality of others, but in order that through understanding he may gain for himself the greatest possible scope, clarity, and certainty; for this reason does not aspire to level and destroy.

Spinoza regarded philosophy as one, and this one as knowable by reason and exclusively true. In this belief, he confused it with science. He was able to convince certain critics (Jacobi, Lichtenberg) that if reason were the foundation of all life, it could lead only to Spinozism. This is a philosophical fallacy. In the study and acquisition of Spinoza we must differentiate:

1. Where he is dealing with scientific questions, he is fundamentally right, though not in detail. Even this is valid only for those who strive without restriction for science, who regard a bond with scientific possibilities as the condition of all integrity, who take an affirmative attitude toward science and find human dignity in pursuing it. Those who are unwilling cannot be convinced, because they close themselves off from thought and communication is broken; there is nothing for it but to leave them to themselves. Unconditional support of scientific truth is an element of philosophical faith. In this respect Spinoza is one of the long line of men who have worked for knowable truth against error. This attitude has given rise to great transformations in our world view (Copernicus; the discovery of the whole earth, the discovery of other, entirely different men; realistic history and its extension over unknown millennia). Where such changes are felt to be unbearable, the old truths that they put in jeopardy cannot be

defended from the standpoint either of sound knowledge or of communicable universality.

2. Where philosophy is concerned, Spinoza, after the manner of philosophers, expresses the truth which is unconditional in his own life as a thinker, but which once formulated is not universally valid for all.

These two concepts of truth are different in origin. Science is concerned with a truth that is universally valid; but this truth is inseparable from certain specific methods and definable premises; it is always particular and in actual fact comes to be accepted by all who understand it. Philosophy is concerned with a truth which in its statement does not become universally valid, which in practice does not gain universal acceptance, but comes from a source that is taken as an absolute.

A consequence of this distinction between science and philosophy is that their opposition to the theology of any church takes two fundamentally different forms. Science opposes theology insofar as it makes statements about realities in the world or hands down supposedly logical demonstrations, which in both cases can be compellingly refuted to the satisfaction of every thinking mind. In this realm theology regularly gets the worst of the argument and tends to adapt itself. Philosophy also opposes theology, but not in reference to particular positions; what philosophy attacks is the authority of its ground. While in the first case better knowledge triumphs over ignorance, in the second case philosophical faith opposes ecclesiastical-authoritarian faith. When philosophical faith, which gains self-certainty in thinking from the source, takes itself for science, it is in error and soon comes into a position of inferiority to theology. When it understands itself on the basis of its own origin, it holds its ground. But then there are not two adversaries, one of whom must triumph; there is a living polarity, inherent in the possibilities of human existence. The independence of science is always particular, relating to the knowledge of those objects that are within its reach. The independence of philosophy is total, relating to the quest for the source of metaphysical and ethical knowledge. The independence of scientific knowledge might be reconciled with authoritarian theological knowledge; but the same can hardly apply to the independence of philosophical faith once its twofold nature has become clear. An example of magnificent original naïveté is Anselm; the first great example of a truly modern philosophical independence is Spinoza.

When orthodox faith and Spinoza's rational insight are considered on the same plane—on the plane of faith, for on no other is such a comparison justified—we see that conflict is inevitable. But a consequence of their divergent origins is that not only their methods of discussion but also their existential implications in the conflict with violence are fundamentally different. Philosophical faith gives battle only intellectually, its attitude toward violence is defensive; theological faith makes offensive use of violence.

Failing to suspect the difference between science and philosophy and hence the ground of his philosophical faith, which he identified with scientific evidence, Spinoza looked upon his philosophy not as the best but as the only true philosophy. This is why he takes such a resolute stand against *skepticism,* which he rejects as pusillanimity. But skepticism can have two meanings: it can mean doubt in the objective and universal validity of philosophical truth, and then it is not pusillanimity, but the force of faith, which has achieved self-awareness by drawing a distinction between scientifically valid statements on the one hand and philosophical statements on the other. Or skepticism can be a doubt in the reliability of our scientific knowledge; in this case it is a force for improved methods in specific branches of inquiry, and here again it cannot be called pusillanimity. Pusillanimous and ultimately nihilistic doubt is the attitude of those who do not live by the earnestness of any form of faith; it is the general attitude of those who assume all science to be uncertain without systematic examination of its particular achievements. Both varieties of skeptical pusillanimity lose themselves in abstract generalizations.

The absoluteness of philosophical insight as Spinoza understood it derives a character of philosophical struggle from its dogmatism. Spinoza recognizes the adversary as a natural necessity; he does not wish to destroy him, but to defend himself against this adversary who threatens his existence. He defends himself by caution and by the publication of his ideas, which, he hopes, will increase the sum of reason in the world. Both Spinoza and his theological adversaries can be accused of intolerance. But Spinoza's intolerance was purely intellectual, brought about by his failure to understand the powers of faith that were utterly alien to him; he was not intolerant in his life, never contemplated violence, and relied only on the power of reason. The intolerance of the theological powers of faith intervenes violently in men's existence, striving to destroy all those who do not comply.

In conclusion it may be asked: Is any discussion possible between powers so different in origin as authoritarian faith, philosophical faith, and scientific knowledge? Is it not inevitable that any attempt of men dominated by one of these powers to address the others will fall on deaf ears? Must all not feel misunderstood, because there is nowhere a "common ground"?

The answer: Scientific and philosophical discussions differ in character. When properly conducted, scientific discussion leads to a compelling result in the realm of the understanding (consciousness as such), which cannot but induce agreement; philosophical discussion, on the other hand, leads to reciprocal illumination in human communication on the basis of something that is common to all men, of men's ability to understand one another amid enduring existential diversity.

Scientific discussion presupposes the common ground of "consciousness as such," which is indeed present in all men. Exceptions occur where a *sacrificium intellectus* is exacted, that is, where the mind is called upon to submit to something that is an absurdity for any thinking man. Here the consequence can only be a common bond in the absurd (while it lasts) or a break in communication. Discussion has become impossible. Men behave as though they were no longer men, that is, thinking beings—and this while invoking something which they assert to be the will of God.

Philosophical discussion requires "correctness" as an indispensable instrument; it operates with scientific knowledge, but its essential aim is something else. The truth of one possible existence enters into communication with another. How this can come about it is hard to explain, for there is no great concrete example in history (except in Plato and Kant, and even so their vision of a community was never realized in practice).

Spinoza could not seek such communication; he was not aware of communication as a task, because he thought himself to be in possession of the true and explicit philosophy.

SPINOZA AS A SCIENTIST

Spinoza took an interest in the modern sciences; he experimented, ground lenses, busied himself with mathematics, and studied medicine. His political thinking is based on Machiavelli. He made a philological and historical study of the Bible, contributed to the dating of various sections by cataloguing the use of certain words and by analyzing indications given in the texts. His work in this field was thorough and conscientious (just as the lenses he ground were said to be of particular excellence). He possessed a modern consciousness of reality.

But he made no outstanding new discovery and no discovery at all in the strict sciences. And though the principles he applied to the study of the Bible have remained virtually unchanged, his own investigations in this field yielded no epoch-making results. It was known before Spinoza that Moses was not the author of the Pentateuch (Hobbes).

Spinoza understood neither the traditional interpenetration of philosophy and science nor the fundamentally absurd marriage between modern science and the philosophy of his time. Not only did he philosophize entirely in the old spirit of the unity of philosophy and science, but moreover, he did not understand the specifically new, modern spirit of science. This becomes evident in his discussion with Boyle, the chemist. It was in the old, scholastic manner (like Bacon) that Spinoza discussed the new facts which Boyle had discovered by new methods, and it was in this manner that he made his own fruitless experiments in connection with Boyle's problem. To be sure, Spinoza understood the endlessness of investigation in the world of modes, stressed our enduring ignorance, and left room for all the new knowledge that could be gained. But his false method of discussion was not in keeping with this insight. For he continued to treat natural science as a fundamentally closed and complete body of knowledge. Formerly it had been the Aristotelians, now it was the Baconians who thought in this manner. His attitude was approximately that in which Siger of Brabant defended the independence of natural science against revelation. Spinoza cannot be included in the great movement of scientists who have worked toward a boundless future that will bring knowledge as yet unsuspected. While Bacon was less interested in scientific progress than in speculations about future technological developments, Spinoza attached little importance to the progress of science, because in his view the essential, the fundamental, the whole was already established: like the ancients, he confused philosophical speculation with scientific knowledge. Thus in its basic attitude Spinoza's natural science is not science in the modern sense, but natural philosophy.

Yet Spinoza was touched by the breath of modern science. He seems to have had modern science in mind when he said that his method of explaining the Bible differs in no way from the method of explaining nature. But in his philosophy all this has the air of a garment that can be changed at will, or of a means of communication which he employs without being committed to it.

The necessity, into which reason has insight as into divine eternity, is expressed through its mathematical and scientific manifestations. Actually Spinoza's use of these new tools does not bear witness to any scientific consciousness and method; as was customary in those days, he employed them as technical aids in a realm unrelated to their own content. This is evident from his use of the geometric method in the *Ethics*. In this work there is no trace of the spirit of mathematical discovery or of the mathematical conception of certainty. But it is quite in the spirit of traditional logical argumentation that Spinoza gives this mathematical cloak to his metaphysical speculations as a means of demonstrating the connections between his concepts. Spinoza's philosophical method of deriving and confirming his ethical views has nothing to do with modern science. The freedom from bias, power of observation, natural intelligence which Spinoza shows in his judgment of reality are not specific to modern science but characteristic of rational human beings at all times. Finally, when Spinoza speaks of the "fictions of Aristotle, Plato, or others of their ilk" and of "Aristotle's buffoonery," it is not in the spirit of the modern sciences, but in the independent spirit of his century, which viewed tradition and great names with suspicion and disrespect.

Though all the thinkers, scientists, and philosophers of Spinoza's time spoke of "method," Spinoza's method is far more a way of salvation than a method of research. When he seeks the way to "improvement of the understanding," it is in order to arrive, by the stages of knowledge, at the intuitive insight of *amor intellectualis dei*.

B. BIBLICAL SCIENCE, FAITH, PHILOSOPHY

1. The importance of Biblical science for faith: Either of the two conflicting assumptions on which Biblical exegesis is based (the Bible as the word of God or as a literary document) can lead to a profound knowledge of the

Bible. In both ways it is possible to read the Bible, to study it, and to reflect upon it. Both are justified in calling themselves Biblical science. But the first assumption implies an acquisition that will sustain the student's whole life, the second a historical knowledge of the meaning intended by the authors, and of the context, origin, and influence of the ideas communicated.

The Biblical science of believers in revelation is as old as the canon. Historical Bible criticism began in the eighteenth century on the foundations laid by Spinoza, and developed enormously in the nineteenth and twentieth centuries. The question arose: What does historical Bible criticism mean to those who believe in revelation? Kierkegaard's answer was: Nothing; historical Bible criticism is detrimental to faith. Few theologians followed him in this belief. Most, sharing the esteem of their age for science, held that historical knowledge of the Bible was useful to the religious reader. Others, however, felt that historical Bible criticism is in itself an expression of unbelief. The same assertion was made from the opposite standpoint by the average proponents of enlightenment: science has refuted Biblical faith. Those historical critics who regarded themselves as believers were faced with a new question: How can faith itself be made more authentic by this new historical knowledge?

Spinoza did not ask the question in this way. Nor could he have done so, for the Bible criticism that he helped to found was not yet an established discipline. He seldom seemed to respect the pious interpretation. He held it to be situated in the realm of the imagination, to be inherently unintelligent, but under certain conditions harmless. As a rule he condemns it in the sharpest terms. It is "a prejudice of superstition to honor the books of Scripture more than the word of God itself." The theological exegetes represent their fictions as the word of God. Under the pretext that religion requires it, they try to compel others to share their opinion. Frivolously and unscrupulously, they squeeze their inventions out of the Holy Scriptures. But their own mode of life shows them to be lacking in piety. Their ambition and profligacy go so far that not "obedience to the teachings of the Holy Ghost, but the advocacy of human fictions is looked upon as the mark of religion," which "consists no longer in love, but in raging hatred."

Nevertheless we are entitled to ask: Can a religious exegesis of the Bible, based on the assumption that the Bible is the word of God, not be reconciled in the mind of a believer with one based on historical inquiry? To be sure, the proponents of the two interpretations cannot carry on a discussion, for they have no common ground. Each can merely point out the consequences of the other's assumptions. One, for example, may say: By denying the uniqueness and holiness of Scripture, you lose God's revelation, you lose what millennia have attested by their faith. And the other may answer: You are turning your back on natural reason, which makes the Scriptures accessible by treating their contents as the opinions of those who wrote them; which, on the basis of all available documents, investigates the historical conditions and origins and shows how the tenets of faith change, how they gain and lose in depth. To relinquish reason is to lose your authenticity by closing your eyes to reality. But in such an exchange both are mistaken. Might not both ways lead to insights that can coexist in one mind without clashing, since they relate to totally different realities, on the one hand the eternal reality of God in faith, on the other, the empirical reality of the Bible as an object of inquiry? The two conceptions of reality become incompatible only when confused and identified.

Spinoza neither asked this question clearly nor answered it. For one thing, he did not clearly differentiate his own rational, philosophical interpretation from the orthodox interpretation, and he distinguished neither of these strictly from a scientific determination of facts or from the (always hypothetical) psychological and sociological theories of the origins of the Bible. Spinoza made such distinctions, to be sure, but he did not hold them fast in developing his ideas.

2. *The importance of philosophy for faith:* Spinoza's distinction between revealed faith and rational insight is a distinction between the realms of theology and philosophy. But did Spinoza really wish to distinguish theology and philosophy as two independent realms of equal rank? Over and over again, he represents reason as the highest criterion. Revelation as an instrument of obedience is held to be a necessity rooted in the nature of most men, but subordinate. There are two planes: the historical plane of man as a finite mode with inadequate ideas and the eternal plane of man as a rational being who, with his adequate ideas, cuts across time, revelation, and tradition, to enter into an immediate relation to God.

In Spinoza's thinking a motive is at work which is at once philosophical and political: the self-assertion of philosophical reason. What is accomplished in the mind of the philosopher is not identical with what is known as reality in the realm of modes. Reason itself becomes a mode in its historical manifestation. The knowledge of the modes of history is finite knowledge, but as such is also a demand of reason.

Spinoza often fails to make clear whether he recognizes revelation as an act of God or whether he is only speaking "according to the comprehension of the multitude." It is certain that Spinoza regards this historical reality of faith, like everything else that exists, as a consequence of God, but this does not mean that he believes in the reality of revelation as a specific act of God, localized in space and in time. This last possibility, even if he sometimes seems to imply it, is philosophically excluded.

Does Spinoza in general fail to establish a systematic connection between his actual philosophy and concrete knowledge in the realm of modes? Or in the present case: does he fail to establish a systematic connection between his denial of revelation and his recognition of revelation? The matter is not made clear. For according to Spinoza's fundamental principles, everything that resides in the realm of modes—and this would include all political and ecclesiastical thinking—is absolutely endless. In the present context he does not speak with the rigor of philosophical speculation. He adopts standpoints and delivers judgments which are relative insofar as they are situated in finite existence and take the form of representations. He strives to advance reason in the world of representations. The result is a lack of clarity, which the reader must correct by interpretation.

Ultimately superstition is so termed only if it leads to conflict, disorder, evil. But when in the form of imaginations, of prophetic proclamation of God's commandments, it contains truth, then in fact, though not as knowledge, it is identical with philosophical practice, with love and righteousness, with harmony and peace. The prevalence of superstition in the organized Biblical religions is shown by their conflicts, their fanaticism, their mutual accusations of heresy, their lust for power. But to what extent the truth of reason is effective through the Bible in these religions is shown by the piety which true believers evince in their actions.

It might be said that for Spinoza superstition ceases to be superstition when its content is in keeping with rational practice. But the connection between superstitious form and true content must be understood on the basis of the human mind's attachment to imaginations or inadequate ideas, and of most men's inability to develop their reason to the point where they are truly governed by it and derive strength from it.

The historical study of the Bible shows how from the very beginning enormous changes occurred in the content of faith—from the Mosaic to the Prophetic to the theological, legalistic religion—and how in each of these the tradition was interpreted and assimilated in a different way. It may be asked how the source lives on through transformations, even through seemingly radical breaks, as exemplified by Jesus, or by Spinoza for that matter. In each new historical situation, amid new social forms and conditions of life, the task, where the source contains truth and has been confirmed as historical reality, is to renew the experience of God's original presence. But no one can devise a plan by which to carry out this task. The only answer lies in the reality of each man's life and thinking.

Spinoza himself takes his place in this history of Biblical religion. His experience of God is akin to Jeremiah's: it suffices that God is. Like the Bible, he knows love of God as love of his neighbor and as righteousness. With all the earnestness of an immemorial tradition, he rejects all embodiments, determinations, limitations of God: thou shalt not make unto thyself any graven image. In Spinoza as in the Bible, God-given reason opposes nature gods, demigods, and demons, which vanish in the face of God's reality. Every abasement of God is forbidden, not by any so-called enlightenment, but by the very idea of God.

Biblical consciousness of God in philosophical form takes Bible criticism as a historical means of approaching the source. No science of the Bible

can impair this consciousness of God. On the contrary, it helps us to redis-
cover the source. It brings us face to face with a great historical unity forged
by catastrophe and suffering, the fundamental experience of a people and
its many extraordinary individuals.

Spinoza sees the historical unity of the Bible; he sees Jesus as one of a
long line of Prophets, as spirit created by spirit, as "the mouthpiece of God."
With his philosophical consciousness of God, Spinoza expounds the meaning that runs through the whole Bible: the one God, in whose faith are
grounded love and justice among men, and who is the foundation of men's
peace, solely because He is.

Bible criticism teaches us to understand the contradictions that occur
throughout the Bible, either as a meaningful unity of polarities in faith or
as a consequence of the changing historical garments through which faith
has passed. A thorough historical knowledge makes the one God shine all
the more radiantly and enables us to accept or reject the whole with greater
clarity.

C. OBJECTIONS TO SPINOZA'S CONCEPTION OF GOD

1. Abstractness: It cannot be denied that the fundamental ideas, in which
Spinoza's idea of God is expressed, are highly abstract. Insofar as this term
is taken as a reproach, it may be replied:

The more abstract a philosophical idea, the more concrete is its metaphysical reality. The more abstract an idea of God, the greater unanimity
can be achieved among thinking believers; for they fill it with their diverse
historical reality.

A thinker who is able with his speculation to strike at the ground of
being addresses every man. But from the standpoint of objects and representations, his ideas become increasingly empty. Those who do not fill in
this emptiness with their own substance cannot help regarding such ideas as
purely abstract, as mere indifferent form. They experience none of their
effectiveness.

Hence the striving to bring God closer in images, figures, myths and
symbols, in rites, ceremonies, cults, and sacred books. These are the source
of historical diversity, but they are also the body of the absolute, its existence
in time, the historicity of origin, tradition, language. This is the realm of the
fairy tales that we hear from childhood on, of the truths that I accept "because
my father told me so."

Spinoza was expelled from his community because of his insistence on
free speech. He drew the consequence: constrained to live without historical
ground, he would find his ground in God Himself. This accounts for
Spinoza's ahistoricism, for his radical abstraction of the Biblical idea of
God, for the earnestness of his determination to make no graven image, to

live without prayer in the pure ether of thought. In this rarefied medium he found the cool yet radiant reality of God that dominated his life. This divine reality, manifest in pure thought, is the focal point at which all merely historical origins, which left to themselves tend to be mutually exclusive and to establish themselves as objective, dogmatic truth, can converge and submit to a higher authority.

In this encompassing area of thought, which as such can never become an actual institutional religion, Spinoza consequently takes two steps:

The first is to the comprehensive Biblical religion, where the diversities between the churches and denominations of the Old and New Testaments disappear, where all find God and all invoke Him with the words "God is one." Objectively considered, the Biblical religions (including Islam) are one big family, but actually, to their own shame, they are, and potentially remain, an area of bloody conflict over shadings of dogma and liturgy and law. As men attain to reason, such formal thinking as Spinoza's can become a bond among them; it need not involve any sacrifice of their historicity, provided that each faith abandons all claim to absoluteness for its contents, conceptions, utterances, and life forms.

The second step leads beyond the forms of Biblical faith to the abstract realm where we come into contact with China and India, and where the words of speculation contain something which each party understands as an echo of its own thinking, but only in the almost inaccessible abstraction which bears within itself and makes perceptible the one concreteness of the absolute historicity of all reality as it is brought about by God.

Spinoza may be said to have made a personal sacrifice of his historicity to the supra-historical. But his sacrifice is painless. In Spinoza there is no trace of the suffering servant of God (Isaiah) or of the sacrificial death of Jesus; in him there is no depth of suffering, but instead equanimity, joy, serenity, beatitude in God's one reality.

2. *The disappearance of transcendence:* Let us once again sum up Spinoza's idea of God with its consequences: God is the immanent cause of the world. All might is God's might. Might is right. Natural laws are God's laws. In man's state of nature as in all nature, nothing is forbidden or decreed. Prohibitions and commandments spring from a common human will, which has power and legislates, effectively, as long as its power endures. As nature, as a mode of substance, all that exists is beyond good and evil. Thus the appropriate attitude of reason is: despise nothing, ridicule nothing, deplore nothing.

Let us construct a pantheistic view of the world. In it we find three factors: the elimination of transcendence; the disappearance of personality in the totality of God-world-Being; the denial of freedom. In opposition, we construct a theistic view: God's absolute transcendence; insistence on the personality as unique, irreplaceable, and of eternal significance; the assertion of freedom and decision.

Where does Spinoza stand? He has been accused of pantheism; his philosophy has been said to be a philosophy of immanence without transcendence. It has been said that in his view God and the world are the same, that the uniqueness of the individual vanishes, that there is no freedom and no purpose.

But this is not true. The personal subject, to be sure, is a mere mode, but it is present as a reality and drawn to God with all the power of loving insight. Freedom seems to be denied, but it is restored in the form of a new concept: and this freedom, which is peace, clarity, and the rational conduct of life, is the very foundation of Spinoza's philosophy.

God's transcendence is attested in Spinoza by His infinitely many attributes; by the transcending of all purposes in a more powerful principle which is necessary and free from purposes; by the infinity of the never known totality of natural laws; by the fact that man is not the center, but only a mode in the world. The world of modes discloses infinitely many things which, without reference to man, attest the independence of this infinite totality as an effect of God. Spinoza's consciousness of God is serene, loving acceptance of the infinity which is God, inner consent, and serene indifference toward all finite things.

But Spinoza's transcendence does not take the form of an irruption into the world from elsewhere or of a revelation to man; it is not present as a divine commandment or mission. Further, there is in Spinoza no absolute ethical injunction to act in the world against the world, no unconditional obligation, no Kantian categorical imperative; for Spinoza's freedom is the action of reason as the natural essence of man; man is not a fundamentally different being, but one natural being among others. Finally, transcendence is for Spinoza not a reference point for eternal decision; for in his view there is no eternal decision in time, and consequently no existential historicity.

Spinoza did not expressly reject these conceptions that we have found lacking in him; they were simply outside his field of vision. It may reasonably be asked, however, whether the alternative between immanence and transcendence is applicable to Spinoza's thinking. For Spinoza's love of God is not a universal love, if by universe we mean the totality of the modes. When Spinoza says *deus sive natura,* he has in mind God as *natura naturans,* not *naturata.* "It is utterly false," he writes, "to suppose that it is my intention to equate God and nature" (taken to mean some mass or matter). By this he means that God "does not manifest Himself outside of the world in an imagined and represented space," but rather, as St. Paul says, that we "live and breathe in God." The pantheist formula "One and All" (*hen kai pan*) would apply to Spinoza only if the "One" preserved its transcendence and the "All" were not interpreted as the totality of finite things.

3. The loss of historicity: The idea of God has been embodied in two opposite ways.

First: God is looked upon as above all temporal and spatial phenomena, history and nature, nations and laws, good and evil, doom and salvation, and men live with this utterly remote God as though He were intangibly near and present. Where God is viewed in this way, it is not possible to invoke Him for one's own advantage, for it is recognized that all things in space and time come from God. When two human adversaries regard each other as men—in reference to this remote God—chivalric combat is possible between them. And even when this is not the case, when a merciless life-and-death struggle takes place (massacres, wars of annihilation, betrayal, Spinoza's "natural right"), there remains nevertheless a fundamental certainty that God is not lost, that whatever happens God will still be with me, and that even the most terrible calamity must originate with God.

Second: God is close at hand; a nation, an ecclesiastical faith claims Him for itself: We are with God, the others are not; we serve God, the others do not. The others are heretics, godless, heathen. There is an absolute cleavage between men, for God is denied the others. Our struggle for existence with these others is God's battle against the enemies of God: We fight for God against false gods (as though this were God's will). The superior truth of our own faith hallows our own interests and strivings for power.

On the one hand, faith in God as the God of all men and of the world; on the other, national or ecclesiastical belief. Both conceptions are in the Bible: universal religion and national religion; universal religion assuredly since the Prophets, possibly since Moses, perhaps even since Abraham. In this polarity of far and near the idea of God achieves clarity. Nevertheless, the process involves two oppositions, which are sometimes equated but are in fact very different:

First: The opposition between universal religion and the historical particularity of its manifestation. History is the middle link in space and time, through which the abstract Encompassing is embodied and handed down in a community, through which it governs every hour and every moment of a man's life.

Second: The opposition between a universal religion and the exclusive pretension of a particular historical embodiment which claims to speak for all mankind: a church calls itself "Catholic," a people claims to be "chosen," it is anticipated that one day all men will worship in Jerusalem.

Both these oppositions are present in the Bible. The substance of the Bible is man's struggle for his eternal reality, which cannot dispense either with historicity or with the all-encompassing one God. Blind to the importance of the historical, Spinoza was entirely on the side of the universal.

This aspect of Spinoza's philosophy reveals its depths and its limits. The supreme abstraction of philosophy actually makes possible the purest historicity. It purifies the historical embodiment of the absolute by stripping its dogmas, views, images, and institutions of false claims to exclusive truth and universal validity.

Spinoza moves entirely on the side of free possibility. The significance of history passed him by. For him, to be sure, the highest abstraction had its greatest power in ethical practice, and this sufficed him. What remains is the equanimity and activity of reason, both free from mythical, dogmatic, legal ciphers. There is in Spinoza a superior truth—but if this truth is to live, it cannot remain an empty abstraction; it must be filled with human existence, which in turn it transforms.

In the year when the anathema was pronounced against Spinoza, Rembrandt's property was sold at auction. Spinoza became an outcast; Rembrandt was socially declassed. Both derived the clarity of their metaphysics from their extreme situation. There is no indication that they ever met.

What Rembrandt saw in created images, and communicates to us in his paintings, Spinoza did not see. Spinoza was without visionary power: even his figures of thought lack the plastic force of symbols. Spinoza had to accentuate this deficiency in himself in order to restore to consciousness and express the full force of the transcendent God, the God who extends over all things, the God before whom there are no demons and gods, no intermediaries. The goal of his thinking was the eternally superordinate, the immutable and intangible, which in Rembrandt's work is the hidden guide but does not stand out as such, because it cannot be embodied in any image and likeness, even though image and likeness are indispensable and become the most moving of languages when they possess Rembrandt's truth.

Perhaps the most noteworthy indication of Spinoza's blindness to the historical embodiment is that while Rembrandt saw the Jewish soul, he himself partook of it but failed to see it. Rembrandt saw the Jewish soul as no one before or after him. And what Rembrandt saw Spinoza did not see. If it is asked where a primordial experience of God such as that which sustained Spinoza, where a life such as that of Jesus, where such power to remain true to oneself in the midst of suffering, where such willingness to draw the extreme consequence, such love, capable of every sacrifice, such fire of the soul is not only conceived of, not only present as an echo, a theoretical interpretation of one's own existence, but utterly real, where men like Jesus (the Jesus of the synoptic Gospels) occur most frequently, we may answer: They are everywhere exceedingly rare, but the most striking examples are among the Jews. With this in mind we shall miss in Spinoza an eye for the Jewish soul, we shall miss the love that perceives such love.

4. The absence of God's fundamental characteristics: In the light of the horrors of human existence, it is argued that the Biblical God is not only unfathomable but also an angry and a jealous God (Thou shalt have no other gods before me), a giver of laws. He is a terrible God. Man knows not only the law of the day, but also the passions of the night; God is manifested in both. But Spinoza denies the jealous God, he takes away God's

sting. He knows only the love, not the fear of God. He cannot understand
the execution of heretics by pious men acting out of a sense of responsibility
to God, nor does he understand the terrible purpose of the anathema ex-
cluding the godless man from the community. Spinoza seeks only appeasement, consolation, and happiness.

In reply to this it can be said: Spinoza perceives the hardness of necessity:
when he looks on as flies are strangled in a spider web, when he senses
the kinship between his thinking and the Calvinist theory of predestination
(though without the concept of sin). But actually Spinoza lives without
fear of the extremes whose existence he states. He rejects fear as irrational.
Fear does not lead to the truth, the goal is equanimity. This criticism
combines heterogeneous factors which have nothing in common but
their irrationality. It cannot be denied that in respect to the passions of the
night Spinoza lacks the openness of reason which, though well aware
that communication with the irrational is in all likelihood impossible,
attempts it nevertheless. In the face of the sufferings and injustices (by
human standards) of existence he is without the spirit of rebellion, which
calls peace of mind an evasion and rejects all veiling of the world's horrors.
He does not know Job's rebellion with God against God, which seeks
salvation not in peace of mind but in God's mercy.

Spinoza, this criticism goes on, disregards the Thou, man's dialogue with
God in prayer. Thus he loses the covenant with God, which is the foundation of both Jewish and Christian life, and with it the self-consciousness of
the historical person, which comes to itself only in dialogue with the
personal God.

Further, it is argued, Spinoza knows only the love of man for God, not
the love of God for man. He tried to prove that "He who loves God cannot
strive that God should love him in return." According to Spinoza, God
loves or hates no one, because He is moved by no affects of joy or sorrow.
However, in speaking of the true love with which *amor intellectualis dei*
and its consequences suffuse our whole attitude toward men and the world,
he said that "God, insofar as He loves Himself, loves men and consequently
that the love of God toward men and the intellectual love of the mind
toward God are one and the same thing."

All these criticisms show a tendency to reject Spinoza. They spring, to
be sure, from the ineradicable drives of finite men, who need the language
of ciphers and historical actuality in space and time. But man can transcend
all these in figures of thought. Spinoza's figures of thought are among the
greatest ever produced and are in turn historical.

When the criticisms spring from an incapacity for such transcending,
they merely bear witness to a failure on the part of the critic. The void opens
before him; Spinoza's overwhelming Encompassing becomes nothingness.
He is closed to the reality which pervades all things in timeless presence, the
reality upon which Spinoza touches in his thinking.

But when the criticisms fixate as an absolute what Spinoza transcends, they disclose a state of mind which reduces men to despair once such fixations (myths, ciphers, dogmas) lose their effectiveness, a despair which can be overcome only by the existential enactment of Spinoza's transcendent idea.

In these criticisms, images and metaphors, which are indispensable to us men, are taken for the reality itself. They identify God with the Less, rather than with the More which Spinoza caught sight of in his thinking.

Those who raise such criticisms decline to participate in the great historical process whereby the Biblical idea of God has undergone continuous purification. In this process Spinoza, like Jesus, played a vital part as one of the true prophets, who have taken seriously the second commandment—Thou shalt not make unto thee any graven image or any likeness—for though it is beyond human strength to fulfill this commandment, without the idea expressed in it every form of belief in God becomes superstition. The Bible laid the foundations of a faith which rejects the falsehood residing in a confusion or amalgamation of belief in God with belief in sacred books, rites, cults, nations, churches, or sacraments. Spinoza was one of the world's truly pious men.

Still, his critics may be right in saying that Spinoza neglects the middle links which connect man, in the finiteness of his thoughts and imaginations, with God. Spinoza took the step to supreme transcendence whither, as he knew, only few can follow. He did not take part in the difficult task of helping, in the community of men, to transmit images and metaphors and to influence the structure of life. The supreme abstraction of thought is indeed unique. It can form a bond between all those who understand it. It provides a horizon in which a historical embodiment can no longer be absolutized, but in so doing it takes no account of historical reality as the temporal fulfillment of existence in its incalculable diversity.

To keep the Biblical consciousness of God alive in this horizon, to reawaken it in its diverse manifestations amid the ever-changing conditions of human existence—that is the great task of the practicing priest. In this task Spinoza took no part. But he did reopen a horizon in which all embodiments can meet one another in communication. The unity of the diverse historical modes of faith becomes perceptible as a center, which finds an expression and index not directly but indirectly through philosophical abstraction.

D. SPINOZA'S DESTINY AND PERSONAL DECISIONS

In the course of his life Spinoza made decisions which determined his personal destiny and were also of fundamental historical importance. The reality of his life became a symbol by which many men in a new age have oriented themselves, some taking it as a model, others as an antitype. It is not possible to think with Spinoza without coming into personal contact with him.

Spinoza combined the Jew's experience of homelessness (his ancestors had been driven out of Spain, his parents emigrated from Portugal to Holland), Spanish culture and Jewish tradition, humanistic education and new philosophy, and finally the political consciousness of a citizen of Holland, to which he remained loyal in his thoughts and actions.

The crucial event of his life was the excommunication, his exclusion from Jewry. Both the Synagogue and Spinoza wished to avoid it. Spinoza claimed the right to remain a member of the Synagogue even if he thought what he held to be true and said what he thought, even if he did not attend divine services or perform the prescribed rites. Spinoza recognized both revelation and reason. It was because they conflicted that he left the Synagogue. He was not permitted to remain under the conditions he demanded; on the contrary, he was abused for his "loathsome blasphemies against God and Moses" (presumably his thesis that the Pentateuch was not written by Moses) and for his "monstrous acts" (no doubt, his disregard of the Jewish ceremonial law).

But why did Spinoza attach so much importance to membership in the Synagogue that he protested the anathema in a work of self-justification (which has not been preserved)? Evidently because of the possible consequences for his civic rights. On the strength of his excommunication, his sisters seem to have contested his right to his paternal heritage. It is certain, in any case, that Rabbi Morteira wrote the Amsterdam magistrate that Spinoza's views on the Bible were also hostile to the Christian religion, and consequently demanded Spinoza's removal from the city. The pastors of the Reformed Church agreed. Spinoza was actually banished from Amsterdam for a few months. He went to Ouverkerk, where he lived under the protection of the municipal authorities. Shortly before, a fanatical Jew had made an attempt on his life, which Spinoza had escaped by his quickness and presence of mind. He saved the coat in which the dagger had cut a hole.

Which of the two parties was in the right? No answer is possible, for their premises are irreconcilable. Spinoza carried the matter to the Dutch civil courts and so obtained protection; the religious question was a matter of indifference to him.

On his exclusion from the Jewish community, Spinoza did not become a Christian. He was friendly with the Collegiants, but his conduct had nothing in common with that of many Jews who were converted to Christianity. We possess no documents relating to Spinoza's motives. But clearly it was impossible for him to participate in a community of faith into which he had not been born. For his philosophy was itself a form of faith in God. He required no religious denomination.

Spinoza desired peace in the beatitude of *amor intellectualis dei.* But inevitably the step he took became a public act. He did not try to sidestep his destiny. What would have happened if he had avoided the break, if he had continued to observe the forms with skeptical indifference? For him, who was not skeptical in the least, this would have meant a life of perpetual dishonesty. It would have been impossible for him to think his philosophy, to write the *Ethics* and the *Theologico-Political Treatise.* He would have become what innumerable others had already been. But might he not have waited and written his philosophy first? No, his thinking was possible only if he could enjoy free speech and refrain from attending divine services. And so, before any of his work came into being, he compelled the Synagogue, by his philosophically so self-evident demands, to expel him. And in all likelihood it was this event which first gave him the full clarity of his philosophy and the will to communicate it to all those who wished to live as free men in the certainty of God.

When Spinoza's reason brought him into conflict with the institution representing his people and church, when in consequence he was rejected by his coreligionaries, relatives, and countrymen, did he fall into a void? No, in an age when every man found spiritual shelter in the authority of his church, an age which for a hundred years had witnessed bloody wars of religion, an age in which the multiplicity of faiths cast doubt upon the truth of faith as such, in which skepticism and unbelief were openly expressed, but in which most men vacillated or with sovereign skepticism paid lip service to church and state, Spinoza dared, with unflagging resolution and the serene self-confidence of one for whom no other choice was possible, to choose a realm which every thinking man is free to enter, where every man can be at home regardless of his origins or tradition, which cannot be taken away, the realm of God's reality manifested in the certainty of reason.

Was Spinoza at home anywhere else? He was a Dutchman. But though he felt obligated to Holland for giving him the citizenship which made him a free man, Holland was not in the deeper sense his home. Spinoza believed Dutch citizenship to be a sufficient foundation for his living-in-the-world. Holland protected him against the consequences of his excommunication by the Synagogue. Though in those days Holland was free only in comparison with the other European states of the time, though he was still in such danger that when he did publish a book it was with great hesitation, he was nevertheless grateful: "To us has been granted the rare good fortune to live in a state where each man is accorded full freedom to judge and to worship God as he sees fit, a state in which freedom is looked upon as the most cherished and precious of treasures."

Spinoza's sober view of the nature of the state was in keeping with this situation. His state is far from Platonic. Nor is it ecclesiastical; it has no religious foundation, but requires, as the conditions of peace and freedom, tolerance toward all faiths and denominations. It is not absolutist as in

Hobbes, but liberal, allowing for contending opinions. It has no pedagogic function, but is solely a community of law aiming at the freedom of all. Nor is the state ethnic, for it is based on a purely political principle.

In view of the realities of those times it may be asked: How is it possible that a man who had expressed such opinions as Spinoza should have been treated so mildly? One would have expected him to be destroyed or banished. The reasons were these: He was a Jew, not a Christian. Thus in Christian eyes he was not a heretic, for he had not fallen away from Christianity. Had he been a Christian, the Church authorities would have had the power to persecute him in earnest. His excommunication by the Jews was of little interest to the Christians. Moreover, Spinoza lived quietly, unobtrusively. His personality aroused sympathy even in his opponents. He made no propaganda, never engaged in active rebellion. Resolute as he was in his philosophy, he was never provocative or insulting in his personal conduct. Finally and above all, he had a keen sense of reality and was very careful.

E. SPINOZA AND THE JEWISH QUESTION

1. Our question. As a Jew Spinoza had already encountered the experience of exclusion. But in addition he was excluded from Jewry. His destiny seems to foreshadow the uprootedness forced on many men in the modern world and to set an example of how a man can bear himself in this situation. He himself is famous as the great, remarkable, or abominable Jew. We cannot help looking for Jewish motives in his thinking, for the influence of Jewish religious and political sentiment on his way of life.

In Spinoza such a question finds no answer. He never tells us that he felt himself to be a Jew. His origin was not a matter of essential importance to him. He was not conscious of any Jewish question. He looked upon the persecutions of the Jews without emotion, as an objective historical observer. He could not suspect what the Jewish question was to become in the second half of the nineteenth century. Nor did his theologico-political thinking lead him to conceive of any such thing as Jewish "rights"; in general he had no notion of the political rights of man.

What would Spinoza say in the present situation? The modern Jew and every man who felt the shock of the extermination of the Jews by Hitler's Germany must ask himself: What shall I do if my fellow men suspend my civil rights, persecute me, and set out to destroy me because of my demonstrable origins (religion, race, class)? Spinoza would reply by referring to the natural principle of self-assertion, not by appealing to eternal justice or invoking any right. Only one thing can help: the self-assertion of those who are persecuted by their fellow men and compelled by this same persecution to become a community.

Spinoza would add that this has no more to do with God than any other self-assertion. For all spring from His eternal necessity. Spinoza would not equate this assertion of a people's existence with a covenant which God concluded with the Jews. He would not identify the sheltering certainty of God's existence with belief in a God who gave my people and myself guarantees for existence. Even in the face of the destruction of his own people, he would say with Jeremiah: "The Lord saith thus: Behold, that which I have built will I break down, and that which I have planted I will pluck up. . . . And seekest thou great things for thyself? seek them not. . . ." Spinoza would say that in a situation of threat the concept "Jew" embraced believers and unbelievers alike, who belong together because and insofar as they are marked by demonstrable historical origin and are united by the threat and reality of extermination.

Spinoza would see only the struggle for existence under the natural right which alone prevails, where peoples wish to live and to live in their own way, and desire freedom because they are not barbarians. No people's right is greater than its might. Peoples live by the same right as fishes—the larger eat the smaller.

Hence there is no superordinate authority which guarantees my rights. For right exists only in the state and through the state, as far as its might extends. The superordinate authority is all-encompassing divine necessity, in which everything that happens has its place. It is above all civil laws, which are valid only in states. The particulars of this authority of divine necessity cannot be inferred from any known natural law (for complete knowledge is situated in the infinite). Man can only do his best and accept what happens in accordance with the supreme authority of divine necessity. Thus destiny remains hard and terrible and ambivalent, and Spinoza's only response to this destiny is equanimity based on certainty of God's existence. But philosophical insight cannot countenance the delusion that there exists any halfway reliable superordinate authority to guarantee right. All arguments seeking to derive a right without might are mere self-deception. They inspire the mightless with feelings of resentment, unjustified because based on the principle of a nonexistent superior right, through which the impotent expect to gain prestige and power. Or on the side of the mighty, eager to increase their momentary power, such arguments encourage an unwarranted belief in a principle of legitimacy based on superior value (race, election, descent from the gods). They strive to enhance their real power by marking its holders with a character of eternal superiority and merit. Both delusions blind those who harbor them to the realities which in both cases are those of natural right, and so cause both the mighty and the mightless to neglect the measures necessary to the assertion of their existence. Such self-exaltation induces confusion through inadequate ideas, or affects, and invariably leads to disaster.

2. *Spinoza on the Jews*. But Spinoza himself spoke of the destiny of the Jews. This is his view:

Moses established the Hebrew state by his covenant with God. "God alone held dominion over the Hebrews, whose state, by virtue of the covenant, was called God's kingdom, and God was said to be their king; consequently the enemies of the Jews were said to be the enemies of God, and the citizens who tried to seize the dominion were guilty of treason against God; and, lastly, the laws of the state were called the laws and commandments of God. . . . Civil and religious authority were one and the same. The dogmas of religion were not precepts, but laws and ordinances. . . . Anyone who fell away from religion ceased to be a citizen and on that ground alone was accounted an enemy." This specific historical condition had extraordinary consequences for the inner attitude of the Hebrews. "The love of the Hebrews for their country was not mere patriotism, but also piety, and was cherished and nurtured by daily rites until, like their hatred of other nations, it must have passed into their nature." Not only was the daily cult of the Hebrews entirely different from the cults of other peoples; it was also directed against them. "Such daily reprobation naturally gave rise to a lasting hatred, deeply implanted in the heart: For of all hatreds none is more deep and tenacious than that which springs from extreme devoutness of piety, and is itself cherished as pious." Other peoples responded with hatred to the hatred of the Jews, which was thus further enhanced.

Spinoza believed the situation of the Jews to be entirely different in his day. Since the loss of their state, he held, the Hebrews exist only through their religion. "Today, there is absolutely nothing that Jews can arrogate to themselves beyond other nations." "As to their continuance so long after dispersion and the loss of empire, there is nothing marvelous in it, for they so separated themselves from every other nation as to draw down upon themselves universal hate, not only by their outward rites, which conflict with those of other nations, but also by the sign of circumcision which they most scrupulously observe." Spinoza regarded the sign of circumcision as "so important that I could persuade myself that it alone would preserve the nation for ever."

He believed that he could prove by the events in Spain and Portugal that the chief reason for the survival of Jewry was the hatred of other peoples: "When the King of Spain compelled the Jews to embrace the state religion or go into exile, a large number of Jews accepted Catholicism. Now, as these renegades were admitted to all the native privileges of Spaniards and deemed worthy to fill all honorable offices, they soon became so intermingled with the Spaniards as to leave of themselves no relic or remembrance. But exactly the opposite happened to those whom the King of Portugal compelled to become Christians, for they always, though converted, lived apart, for they were considered unworthy of civic honors."

Spinoza understands the "election" of the Jewish people as applying only to their native country and material welfare. "If anyone wishes to maintain that the Jews, from this or from any other cause, have been chosen by God for ever, I will not gainsay him if he will admit that this choice, whether temporary or eternal, has no regard, insofar as it is peculiar to the Jews, to anything but dominion and physical advantages (for by such alone can one nation be distinguished from another), whereas in regard to intellect and true virtue, every nation is on a par with the rest, and God has not in these respects chosen one people rather than another." But today, says Spinoza, they have lost the land of Palestine. Their election is suspended. Yet Spinoza thought the Jews would probably survive. "I would go so far as to believe that if the foundations of their religion have not emasculated their minds they may even, if occasion offers, so changeable are human affairs, raise up their empire afresh, and that God may a second time elect them."

3. Spinoza's political attitude toward the Jewish question. Spinoza, whose ancestors had been driven from Spain, whose parents had emigrated from Portugal to Holland, never said a word in anger or accusation about the persecution of the Jews, never invoked the rights of man in their behalf. He felt no desire to help his people. They were prospering in Holland. The Synagogue was influential enough to persuade the Dutch authorities to banish Spinoza from Amsterdam. Spinoza was gravely threatened by the Jews (although the attempt on his life cannot be imputed to the Synagogue) and protected by a state constituted in freedom for freedom. Because the Jews in Holland were not in danger, Spinoza was aware of no immediate occasion to reflect on the future and the destiny of the Jews. The religion of the law and the ceremonies were matters of indifference to him.

As far as the security and rights of the Jews in Holland are concerned, Spinoza's view has been magnificently borne out. Never since the sixteenth century have the Jews in Holland been persecuted, never have their rights been impaired. When Hitler Germany was committing its crimes against Dutch Jews and the non-Dutch Jews living in Holland, the small, powerless country, though unable to save most of them, did more to protect the Jews than any other of the countries overrun by Hitler—with the exception of Italy.

4. Spinoza's abandonment of his bond with Jewry. The Jews, but not Spinoza, lived by the covenant which their people had made with God through Moses, which gave them confidence that insofar as they obeyed God they would, as the chosen people, find happiness also in earthly existence. They interpreted the calamities that struck them as God's punishment for disobedience and questioned themselves as to their guilt. But then it became evident to those Jews, who in accordance with God's commandment revered the truth above all else, that the pious were far from being always rewarded or the godless always punished. Thus Job disputed with God for God's justice, but recovered his confidence when overwhelmed by the word of God, who provides no answer to the question, who does not untie the knot, but gives satisfaction by the mere fact that He is. We may ask: Is Spinoza's certainty of God a modified form of this Jewish certainty? Did his eternal necessity replace the unfathomable?

Spinoza dropped the ceremonial laws, the Messianic idea, the covenant; did he not thereby drop all reality in the world, so that nothing remained but the area in which an individual lives as an individual? The butt of Spinoza's antagonism was not Jewry but the Synagogue. He rebelled against the restriction on freedom of thought and the constraint of the ceremonial laws, against censorship and intolerance. The conflict of his youth was enhanced by his question as to the nature and conditions of freedom, by his meditation on the state, in which each man is allowed to think as he sees fit and to say what he thinks. This was not merely a Jewish question, but the great question of the Occident and ultimately of mankind, to whom Spinoza addressed his grandiosely simple words.

I cannot agree with those who speak of the "hard, nay hostile judgments which Spinoza made against the people from which he issued" (Gebhardt). His tone is no different than when he speaks of Christian affairs. He was radical in his judgment of all revealed religion; to him it was self-evident that the Old and the New Testament must be taken together as documents of a progressive religious experience; he had the same words of violent condemnation, "insane," etc., for both Christian and Jewish fanaticism.

Spinoza was cognizant of no bond of any kind with Jewry. His thinking has its ground solely in human reason, not in any presupposed historical substance of Jewry (though from our point of view, he is very much a part of this substance). In Spinoza we find no trace of a claim to his ancient heritage. Neither in his evaluations nor in his affections did he show any preference for his own people. He had no feeling for the ideas of election or of the covenant as ciphers for a demand not on others but of the Jews upon themselves. He seems to have been blind not only to the rich history of his people but also to their depth of soul, which was the source of his own. Spinoza combated the philosophy of Maimonides because of its ties with Judaism; it never occurred to him that the historical bond of a Jew with the Jewish people could be of an entirely different nature.

Despite his extraordinary philosophical radicalism, Maimonides speaks as a pious Jew to pious Jews (Leo Strauss). He assumed that the Bible can be understood in terms of reason (and to this end employed the allegorical interpretation, which Spinoza condemns as fictitious). He further believed that revelation was necessary on rational grounds and could be understood in terms of reason. He did what the Moslem Averroës and the Christian Anselm did in their own way: he found reason in revealed faith itself. "Born as a Jew among Jews, he carried out his argumentation for them in the context of Jewish life."

If Maimonides wrote a critique of revelation on the basis of revelation, Spinoza criticized revelation on the basis of the God-confident reason that is innate in all men. Spinoza also recognized the historical and political function of revelation, but he did not presuppose revelation on the strength of his own belief. Spinoza submitted Judaism, as he did all things human, such as Christianity and the state, to the highest authority, that of philosophical reason.

5. Judgments concerning Spinoza as a Jew. Nietzsche's love and deep respect for Spinoza did not prevent him from criticizing him: "Hatred of the Jews corroded the Jewish God"—a statement for which there is not the slightest justification in Spinoza. Spinoza neither hated nor loved the Jews, and in general he loved no groups or peoples, but only God and man as man.

The anathema of the Synagogue (one must read it with its blood-curdling curses) has led all orthodox Jews to reject Spinoza. But it seems strange that Hermann Cohen, a German professor of philosophy, should have judged no differently. Cohen regarded the excommunication of Spinoza as absolutely justified, "quite regardless of the need to protect the community against the informer type so prevalent in the history of Jewish persecutions." For Spinoza remains "the true accuser of Jewry before the Christian world." He "rejected the religion in which he was born, casting ignominy upon his own people." He completed "the annihilation of the religion from which he issued." He set Christ above Moses (Spinoza made no such statement; Cohen must have inferred it). Spinoza's influence has been monstrous: "The orgies of anti-Semitic hatred" in the nineteenth century "would be inexplicable if the evil spirit of Spinoza had not inwardly and outwardly poisoned the atmosphere." Cohen became the prototype of the modern Spinoza hater. Strange to say, Franz Rosenzweig, who is not without merit as a philosopher, supported Cohen's judgment, though in a somewhat attenuated form.

Most nonorthodox Jews have taken a very different view. They are proud of this great Jew. In the three hundredth year after the excommunication a block of granite was sent to The Hague from Israel with the inscription: "Your People." Spinoza would have been surprised. He never thought in terms of his people. No people, no state, can lay claim to a man of Spinoza's rank. A Jew, to be sure, is entitled to feel that in all likelihood only Jewry was capable of producing a man like Spinoza. A Dutchman is entitled to feel proud that Spinoza regarded his love of freedom as Dutch and at the same time his own, and that Holland made it possible for him to live. But great men are a challenge, not a possession. Peoples and states must themselves ask whether they have a right to the great men who have come forth from among them. The only appropriate answer is to recognize the standards of these great men as their own.

IX. CRITICAL CHARACTERIZATION OF
SPINOZA'S PHILOSOPHY

A. *A glance at Spinoza's philosophy and character*

1. Rationalism. Spinoza appears to be the most thoroughgoing of rationalists. But it is a strange fact that although in Spinoza compelling logical thought expresses the absolute and is itself authentic reality, this thought is *amor intellectualis dei* and as such beatitude. This thought is freedom from passions which, when elucidated by it, cease to be passions. It is not, like finite thinking, content to apprehend objects which are modes, but finds its completion as reason in the third class of knowledge, in the free speculation of loving intuition. Such thinking was bound to be more than the compelling logical thought which on the surface it always remained. Spinoza transcended thought, insofar as thought is taken as a universally valid operation with fixed concepts. His thinking is a new form of the age-old philosophical contemplation which is an inner action and shapes the whole man.

We have encountered Spinoza's mode of fundamental certainty, built on rational proofs. Let us recapitulate in Spinoza's own words: "Once I am in possession of a reliable proof, I cannot fall back into such ideas as ever to make me doubt this proof. Consequently I am perfectly satisfied with what my understanding shows me, without the least anxiety that I might have been mistaken in it. . . . And even if I should once mistakenly invent the fruit that I have gained from my natural understanding, it would still make me happy, because I strive to spend my life not in sorrow and grief, but in peace, joy, and serenity, and so rise up by degrees. In so doing I recognize (and this is what gives me the greatest satisfaction and peace of mind) that everything so happens through the power of the most perfect being and of His immutable decision."

Spinoza lived and thought on the basis of the fundamental certainty for which God's reality is present in the third class of knowledge as the one all-embracing reality. Starting from this reality, Spinoza takes three courses in the world: to metaphysical knowledge, to personal existence, to the political order. In the language of the second class of knowledge, he develops the communicable knowledge of the totality of Being, of God, the world, and man. By investigating man's affects he finds the way to liberation from them, the happiness and salvation of man through pure insight. In viewing the reality of human society, he investigates the state and revealed religion, in order to set forth an ideal frame in which all human potentialities may unfold in accordance with reason.

2. *The independence of Spinoza's philosophy.* This self-conscious rational thinking was Spinoza's life. He was the only one among the great philosophers of the seventeenth century to build his whole life on philosophy without the security of authority and revealed faith, without any misleading concessions to the powers of the time. He was the great, truly independent thinker representative of the Occident, who found in philosophy what churchgoers called their faith. In him was renewed the independence of philosophy, which has no need of ecclesiastical faith, because it is itself faith.

Such philosophy has been called "philosophical religion" in contrast to ecclesiastical religion. In this sense the great philosophy of antiquity was religion, and in this sense all metaphysics is religion. But in using this word we must not forget that philosophical religion has neither cult, nor prayer, nor institutions, nor Church. Like "philosophical faith," "philosophical religion" refers to a thinking with which and by which philosophical man lives, so that everything he does, everything that happens to him, everything he knows, is brought into this area, is illumined, assimilated, and judged from this source.

Pascal wrote: "God can never be the end of a philosophy if He was not its beginning." So it was with Spinoza. Spinoza thinks in the source, because he is certain of it before all else. He does not rise up from the world (through investigation pressed to the limits) to derive the ground. Nor is it only in extreme situations that he glimpses a cipher of Being, which provides us with a wavering light. Before all investigation of things and all experience of the failure of thought in extreme situations, he is sheltered in the all-embracing reality of God.

Through certainty of God, this philosophical religion of Spinoza brings peace, joy, acceptance of everything that is. "Insofar as we understand that God is the cause of sorrow, we rejoice." From the consciousness of necessity arises the serenity which demands nothing. *Amor intellectualis dei* leads to Nietzsche's *amor fati:* to desire nothing to be different from what it is. From the very beginning, from his first utterance, this miraculous peace is present, this purity of soul, this freedom from purpose even in his volition.

Spinoza's philosophy means the self-assertion of the individual through his experience of God, it means independence of the world through security in the ground of all things. This self-assertion is not individualist preoccupation with his own existence; there is no inclination toward egocentric reflection, but instead the most perfect devotion, in reason, to God. Nor does it mean withdrawal into his own existence from the reality of human society; his interest in mankind was just as great as—but no greater than—his interest in his own existence.

Thinking oriented toward the well-being of the individual and political thinking go hand in hand. But here there is no cult either of the state or of the individual. The realities of practical life are seen with sobriety. But this sobriety itself springs from *amor intellectualis dei,* which does not allow him to set anything else in God's place or to forget the hierarchical orders of reality, but compels him to keep always in mind the all-embracing eternal reality.

3. Caution and solitude. From the very beginning Spinoza's philosophy was ethos. This is attested by the explanation that he gave in his youth for his decision to take up philosophy, and by the title of his main work, the *Ethics.* We have tried to show the depth of this ethos. It includes features that do not spring from Spinoza's innate being but are a consequence of Spinoza's contact with the world.

Caution: Despite the love of God that was present in Spinoza's whole view of the world, despite the benevolence he felt toward every man he met, Spinoza also felt keen distrust; for he knew the reality of the world. Hence his caution without defiance or blame.

Spinoza gave freely of himself but did not squander his strength: he was on his guard against negligence, and reasonably so, for he knew the harm that can spring from it.

He renounced all idea of fame. Even academic activity involved too much danger in those days, and so he declined it. He delayed publication of his works, but he wrote them—without haste—in the hope of broadening the scope of reason in the world.

Not a recluse, but solitary: Spinoza was formerly regarded as a recluse. The studies of the last half-century have exploded this legend. Not only was Spinoza in touch, through friends and acquaintances, with the whole cultural world of Europe, but he also took part in political activity. There was nothing of the eccentric about him; wherever he went his bearing was easy, natural, noble; he was not only respected, but loved as well.

It is a different matter to say that Spinoza was a solitary man. In his philosophizing he gained a "standpoint outside," in God, and he did not relate his philosophy to worldly affairs. On the one hand he was perfectly independent thanks to his certainty of God, on the other hand he had many human contacts which sufficed him, but did not take away his solitude. The consequence is that for us Spinoza seems to lack the love which unites men in their uniqueness, which through companionship and community of destiny leads to unconditional historical commitment. Spinoza was always himself. And what he thought and set forth was the universal, the cool but utterly satisfying realm of thought, the *amor intellectualis dei,* which was his life itself in its highest aspect, in reason. In conversation Spinoza must have been very different from Kant or Max Weber, for example. His almost superhuman calm would elate us. Imperturbable in all situations, he would speak from the standpoint of eternal truth. He would not concern himself seriously with actual realities, but pass them over as nonessential. We should sit in silence, increasingly aware of our own rebelliousness against fate.

4. Neither prototype nor exception. Did Spinoza wish to be a model and prototype? We have no reason to suppose so. Did he wish to show future generations the way? He did not think in historical, reformist perspectives. He wished to live and work in reason, uncertain as to what would come of it.

Or did he regard himself as an exception, condemned by the conflict between his own nature and the existing order to suffer a repugnant fate? No, this too was not the case. He was confident of the natural and appropriate character of his living and thinking. In his work as in his life, he was a healthy, normal man, free from psychological upheavals and crises, free from the endless reflection that drains the mind, never touched by despair in the presence of the void (his illness, tuberculosis, was purely physical; it was able to carry him off at any early age, but not to affect his nature). He must have incurred eclipses of reason, he must have experienced the affects, of which he spoke so knowingly, but only as passing states that vanish once they are understood.

5. The ideas that Spinoza borrowed. The origin of nearly all Spinoza's ideas can be determined: from the Stoics he took his attitude of equanimity based on reason, from the Bible the one God, from Scholasticism such concepts as substance, attribute, mode, of *natura naturans* and *natura naturata*, from Giordano Bruno the infinity of the cosmos, from him and Leo Hebraeus the doctrine of Eros, from Bacon empirical method and the rejection of prejudices, from Descartes the distinction between extension and thought and his regard for mathematical certainty, from Machiavelli and Hobbes his political thinking. It might appear as though Spinoza's entire thinking could be derived from someone else. But Spinoza's thinking is authentic and spontaneous, and his highly original work fused all these rationally definable elements into the language of the One. The totality of this thinking, the fundamental insight, is present from the first. There is development only insofar as the figures of thought are imperceptibly modified, more richly elaborated, clarified and purified. There are no breaks or reversals.

It has been said that with Spinoza for the first time reason stands on its own foundation. But this had long been the case in the "science," the "critique" and "unbelief," that characterize the Renaissance. Spinoza had little in common with this aggressive independence, which for the most part was poor in faith. His thinking was more a continuation of ancient philosophical reason, now clothed in the garments of modern science and critique, and constructed as metaphysical reason. The meaning and aim of knowledge were not for Spinoza the multiplicity of experience and the technical mastery of the world (Bacon), not mathematically intelligible nature (Galileo), not the state (Hobbes), not certainty as such (Descartes), but all these, yet in the service of the One which alone is important, of certainty in God and ethical practice, of the true good.

If we wish to understand Spinoza, we must make no mistake. His foundation is not that of modern science whose nature and method he did not really know (even though the sciences received powerful impulses from certain of his insights, such as his idea of an infinite, never to be completed progression whereby we gain knowledge of the modes in their endless multiplicity and his insistence on freedom from values). He himself was not a scientist and did not possess the scientist's immense capacity for factual knowledge. Spinoza was blind to the special character of exact science and hence ignored it. He did not base his philosophizing on mathematics, even though he employed a supposedly mathematical method of expounding it. He was also a stranger to the spirit of construction, which made Hobbes and Leibniz such great builders and so inventive. Though all these thinkers provided him with ideas, these ideas were incorporated into *his* metaphysics. It is great because it is authentic and one with his life. He thought necessity in rational concepts subservient to the intuition of his third class of knowledge. He is the only great metaphysician of modern times; both in his life and in his work, his style is simple, clear, convincing—and inimitable.

B. *Spinoza's limitations*

1. False criticism. Spinoza has been called a paid propagandist in the service of Jan de Witt. Such nonsense deserves no refutation.

Spinoza has been called a naturalistic, atheistic, amoral philosopher and a precursor of Marxism. But nature in Spinoza is neither the nature of a modern, mechanical, mathematical physics, nor an organic, teleologically structured nature, nor a demonic, sympathetic world; it is the nature of God, conceived as *natura naturans;* in Spinoza's *"deus sive natura,"* the accent is on God. Spinoza's thinking is so far from atheism that Hegel preferred to call it acosmism, because everything is in God, so that no independent, created world, separate from God, is left. His sober view of the natural realities and of God's reality as beyond good and evil has been misinterpreted as amoralism. Actually his life and work are unswervingly sustained by the living morality of natural reason.

It has been said that as a political thinker Spinoza was interested only in the security of philosophers, in the question: How must state and religion be conceived and actually constructed in order that the wise man may be unmolested in his private life? Epicureans and skeptics may have looked at the state in this light, but neither Plato nor Spinoza. They did not seek to guarantee the security of the philosopher by showing that philosophy and politics are incommensurable and advising philosophers to withdraw from the world (except in particular times and under particular circumstances). They are concerned, rather, with philosophical politics over against blind politics; they have in mind all men and aspire to a state in which all will obtain their proper place and right according to their gifts, insight, and affectivity. The impulse which has been mistaken as a striving for the philosopher's security (which can be safeguarded only by private caution) is rather the impulse to promote reason in the world.

Another criticism is that Spinoza's "Being" is geometrical and static, that time is dismissed as mere appearance. Consequently nature is conceived in timeless mathematical formulas, process is denied and with it history. In the opposite direction a "dynamic" view has been imputed to Spinoza: striving, power, perseverance-in-being and self-assertion, all involved in everlasting change in the realm of modes. These criticisms cancel each other out. Both are right to a certain degree, but they apply only to certain elements in the philosophy, not to its substance. The fallacy of such criticism is to take mere figures of thought for the whole instead of understanding their function for the philosopher's fundamental thought. Although Spinoza's thinking is systematic, it cannot adequately be set forth as a system. It is a simple matter to "refute" it by picking out one systematic view and neglecting the rest. This is to treat philosophy as statement of fact and absolute assertion, as objective and finite knowledge.

2. *The limits of reason.* Spinoza's limits are the limits of reason. Because Spinoza does not seem to see the limits of reason, perhaps reality as a whole is closed to him. This is where the profoundest criticism of Spinoza sets in.

The limits of reason can be seen by reason itself. Spinoza seems to have an inkling of this when, in speaking of the infinity of the modes, he says that our ignorance of the endlessness of finite relationships is everlasting and that so many—in fact, nearly all—particulars are incomprehensible to us. But this ignorance is only a consequence of finiteness. In principle, knowledge of these matters is possible, because everything comes from God and is rational.

Spinoza seems to see beyond reason still more clearly when he considers that all our reason is encompassed in divine necessity and represents our human reason as helplessly at the mercy of the necessity of all nature, which it is powerless to understand. But Spinoza seems to take it for granted that this necessity is also divinely rational. The irrational only appears to be irrational to our finite understanding. The encompassing God is not a dark abyss. He is not accessible by any obscure ways, but only through the light of reason itself, which if it could overcome its bond with the limited mode would understand everything as reason. Our human reason is itself divine reason, but in a limited form. Our reason is itself natural, an element in *natura naturata,* but not encompassed and not threatened and not limited by something that is more than reason, by a god that is above and before reason, source of reason but also of everything else. God in Spinoza is reason itself. His consciousness of God does not transcend reason.

Thus convinced of the absoluteness of reason, Spinoza anticipated a day when all men would necessarily unite in reason—a grandiose assumption, but only in reference to practical endeavor, not as an insight into the universe and mankind as a whole.

Another aspect of Spinoza's belief in the absoluteness of reason was the pure, passionless joy of his awareness of God. To him freedom was freedom from affects, pure unclouded clarity, beatitude. Freedom is not decision, not the basis of destiny.

Finally, Spinoza's rationalism made him despise all feelings of wonderment. A reasoning man tries to understand the things of nature "with wisdom," "not to gape at them like a fool." "If ignorance is removed, amazement is also taken away." Amazement becomes harmful when it induces blind subjection to authority, miracles, and supernatural forces.

3. Blindness to personality and historicity. Spinoza was unaware of the limits of reason.

a) He found no answer to the question: Why are there individuals? For to say that all things "follow" eternally from God (as the sum of the angles of a triangle follows from the essence of a triangle) is not an answer, but a mere statement of the fact that individual things are connected with their source. It is only a metaphor pointing to something that thought cannot fathom, a leap from *logos* to reality. Conceived from the standpoint of eternity, the individual—a mere mode—loses all importance and vanishes.

The statement that *omnis determinatio est negatio* expresses the truth as to the insignificance of individuals, but it also makes possible the error of denying that Existenz derives eternal importance from the irreplaceable character of its embodiment.

Does the renunciation of individuality bring with it blindness to the irreplaceable character of Existenz (though not to the reality of Spinoza's own Existenz)? Liberation from the bonds of individuality might mislead one into sacrificing Existenz in its historicity, into sacrificing that which is eternal in human destiny. As Spinoza states it, eternal immortality of the soul is not very different from the immortality of impersonal reason as such (the *intellectus agens* of Averroës).

b) By negating time, Spinoza destroys historicity. The world ceases to be fragmented by the riddle of time, the depth of historicity, the opaque ground of all things. No longer is it incumbent on us to attain to transcendence in time, through historical Existenz. History loses its meaning as a temporal process that can never be completed, because the weight of Existenz is absorbed by God. There seems to be only eternity, not time, only God and no world.

The weight of action rooted in our situation is lost; there remains only the inner action of loving ascent to God. Spinoza knows necessity, but he does not know uncertainty, hope, and failure in the active historicity of Existenz. Time is effaced, but it should also be preserved, because without it there can be no true consciousness of eternity. There can be no historicity in a life which moves from metaphysics to metaphysics without striking meaningful roots in temporal reality. Historicity is absent when activity is limited to reasonable thinking without a driving will, when the great venture of reason is not experienced as historical destiny. Consequently Spinoza is not attracted by the depth and grandeur which (as in the Jewish Prophets) are still obscure and demand that a man venture all and sacrifice all. Wholly taken up by pure reason as the type of human being and of all being, he is blind to the passions of the night, which to him are mere irrational affects. He is blind to evil.

Spinoza rejected not only the anticipation of an actual Messiah and the corresponding expectation of a second coming of Christ as religious imaginations incompatible with philosophical reason, but also the cipher of Messianic thinking. He had no passion to work actively for the transformation of the world. He knew no hope of a better world grounded in human responsibility. A man who lives in eternity cannot live in the future. God is immutable and His actions are themselves eternal. Immutable is the existence of the infinite modes, though within the unchanging whole all the finite modes are subject to perpetual change.

c) Spinoza knows no extreme situations. He knows no abyss of terror, no despair in the face of the void, no struggle with God, no power of the absurd manifested to reason itself as a positive possibility, no absolutely hidden mystery. His peace is in the positive immensity that is God. But God is seen only in reason and as reason—all horror is reduced to mere inadequate ideas, the irrational, antirational, suprarational are simply thrust aside. And yet they leave man no peace. His certainty in the ground of all things can strike us either as a narrowing of the horizon or as a retreat into the unattainable.

Human nature reacts very differently to extreme situations: it invites suffering, it does not try to withdraw, it regards any attempt at liberation from the overpowering affect as a betrayal. But Spinoza can calmly say of suicides "that they are impotent in mind and have been thoroughly overcome by external causes opposed to their nature." He can declare with complete certainty: "That it is as impossible that a man, from the necessity of his nature, should endeavor not to exist, or to be changed into some other form, as it is that something should be begotten from nothing."

d) Spinoza's joy in existence is without egocentrism but also without the anguish of decision. He lived in the truth of God's reality and the consequence was a reliable selfhood, but this selfhood was not conscious of itself. In opposition to Spinoza it may be asked: Is all the anguish to which man is subjected grounded only in the finiteness of modal being and in inadequate ideas? Or is there a very different anguish relating to the reality of the eternal amid the historicity of our existence? Did Spinoza gain his perfect peace at the expense of the God-related anguish of temporal existence, at the expense of the eternal decision in time? Is there not in this philosophy of necessity an impersonality which is at once moving and dangerous?

e) Because Spinoza was without consciousness of historicity, he was also unaware of the historicity of his own figures of thought. Because he believed that he had conceived the one absolute, compelling truth in a form universally valid for all time, he was a dogmatist. For us the truth of Spinoza does not lie in his dogmatized figures of thought. They themselves are historical symbols; uniquely illuminating, they have become indispensable to us, but they are not objectively absolute.

X. SPINOZA'S INFLUENCE

What carries conviction is not the abstract thought, but the reality lived with this thought. What appeals to us in Spinoza's work is not his solution of so-called objective problems, but the power of philosophical striving for certainty. Men's reactions to Spinoza, as to no other philosopher of modern times, were determined by the philosopher he really was. No other aroused so much warm affection and so much bitter hatred. The name of no other has so unique a ring, no other has been so despised and so loved by Christians and Jews alike. He became almost a mythical figure. No one who knows him can remain indifferent to him, for in connection with Spinoza even expressions of indifference mask a self-protective aggressiveness.

Spinoza had no "school." There have been no Spinozists among professors of philosophy in the sense that there have been Cartesians and Leibnizians. But a furious distaste resulted in incomprehensible injustices and misrepresentations, even on the part of Bayle, who effectively distorted the image of Spinoza for many years to come. Spinoza was the "ill-famed Jew" (Leibniz), he was a "miserable atheist," "a malignant spirit," a "ridiculous chimera" (Malebranche). Down to the second half of the eighteenth century nearly all those who mentioned the name of Spinoza were immediately at pains to disavow him. With few exceptions no one wanted to be associated with him. Even Brucker (1767) speaks of the "scandalous success of Spinoza's godlessness."

Spinoza was first taken up by a few pastors of the Dutch Reformed Church, by mystics, and among artisans in "a movement which stirred up the Dutch people and aroused the Church, and whose after-effects extended into the nineteenth century" (Freudenthal). As late as 1862 there are reports of small groups "in which Spinozist mysticism is the only balm of the soul."

But Spinoza's great influence was on German philosophy and literature. Lessing, Herder, Goethe held him in high esteem. Goethe: "I feel very close to him although his mind was far deeper and purer than mine" (1784). "The figures of this world pass; I should like to concern myself only with the lasting relationships, and so, in accordance with the teachings of Spinoza, gain eternity for my spirit" (from Rome, 1787). As late as 1817 he said that the two men who had most influenced him were Shakespeare and Spinoza. Spinoza, in whom he found "boundless selflessness," gave him "appeasement and clarity."

Kant was scarcely touched by Spinoza, whose work he hardly knew. But German philosophy after Kant was equally influenced by Kant and Spinoza. Jacobi (1785) believed that only Spinoza's philosophy was consistent and thus exposed error and inadequacy. Lichtenberg said the same in a positive sense: "The universal religion will be purified Spinozism. Left to itself, reason can lead nowhere else" (1901). Fichte was fascinated by the system, by the method of strict deduction. He himself took Spinoza as a standard by which to oppose Spinoza: "There are only two fully consistent systems, the Critical and the Spinozist." The Critical system recognizes the limits of the "I am," the Spinozist system surpasses them. Schelling regarded Spinoza as the last philosopher to have concerned himself with the truly great objects of philosophy and showed the greatest regard for him as long as he lived. Hegel regarded Spinoza as absolutely indispensable. "Every thinker must have taken the standpoint of Spinozism, that is the essential beginning of all philosophizing." "Either Spinozism or no philosophy." Kindled by Spinoza, the philosophy of German idealism turned against him.

The influence of Spinoza's Biblical science is without philosophical importance. Actually, few of the theologians who have raised the historical study of the Bible to such magnificent heights ever mention him. Johannes Müller, the physiologist, included a translation of Spinoza's theory of the affects in his once famous *Handbuch der Physiologie des Menschen* (1833–40), but despite this evidence of admiration for Spinoza, he did not make use of his analysis in his own work. Certain psychologists of the nineteenth century mistakenly traced their sterile theory of psycho-physical parallelism back to Spinoza. Here again we cannot speak of a philosophical influence.

BIBLIOGRAPHY

EDITOR'S NOTE:

The Bibliography is based on that given in the German original. English translations are given wherever possible. Selected English and American works have been added; these are marked by an asterisk.

Spinoza

SOURCES:

Spinoza, Benedictus de: *Opera,* ed. by Carl Gebhardt. (Heidelberger Akademie.) 4 vols. Heidelberg, C. Winter, 1925.

*Opera quae supersunt Omnia Benedicti de Spinoza, ed. by Karl Hermann Bruder. 3 vols. Leipzig, Bernhard Tauchnitz, Jr., 1843–6.

*Van Vloten, J.: *Ad Benedicti de Spinoza Opera quae supersunt Omnia Supplementum.* Amsterdam, Fr. Müller, 1862.

*Spinoza, Benedictus de: *The Political Works: The Tractatus theologico-politicus in part, and the Tractatus politicus in full;* ed. and trans. with an introduction and notes by A. G. Wernham. (Latin and English.) Oxford, Clarendon Press, 1958.

*Chief Works of Benedict de Spinoza, trans. by Robert Harvey Monro Elwes. (Bohn's Classical Library edition, 1883.) New York, Dover Publications, 1951.

*Ethics, preceded by On the Improvement of the Understanding, trans. by William Hale White. New York, Hafner Publication Co., 1949 (reprint of 1899 edition).

*Correspondence of Spinoza, trans. by Abraham Wolf. New York, MacVeigh, 1928.

*Spinoza's Short Treatise on God, Man, and His Well-Being, trans. by A. Wolf. London, A. & C. Black, 1910.

Spinoza: *Sämtliche Werke,* trans. into German by O. Baensch, A. Buchenau, and C. Gebhardt. 3 vols. Leipzig, F. Meiner, 1914–22.

Altkirch, Ernst: *Spinoza im Porträt.* Jena, E. Diederichs, 1913; Leipzig, F. Meiner, 1922.

*Colerus, Johannes: *Das Leben des Benedict von Spinoza,* ed. by Carl Gebhardt. Heidelberg, Weissbach, 1952.

Gebhardt, Carl: *Spinoza im Porträt (aus dem Nachlass).* No place, no publisher, 1937.

——: Spinoza: *Lebensbeschreibungen und Gespräche.* Leipzig, F. Meiner, 1914.

*Lucas, Jean Maximilien: *The Oldest Biography of Spinoza,* ed. by A. Wolf. London, G. Allen & Unwin, 1927.

SECONDARY WORKS:

Altkirch, Ernst: *Maledictus und Benedictus: Spinoza im Urteil des Volkes und der Geistigen.* Leipzig, Constantin Brunner, 1924.

*Arnold, Matthew: "Spinoza and the Bible," in *Essays in Criticism.* First Series. London, Macmillan, 1937.

Bäck, Leo: *Spinozas erste Einwirkungen auf Deutschland.* Berlin, Mayer, 1895.

119

*Brunschvicq, Léon: *Spinoza et ses contemporains.* 4th ed. Paris, Presses Universitaires de France, 1951.

*Chartier, Émile A.: *Spinoza.* Paris, Mallottée, 1929.

Cohen, Hermann: "Spinoza über Staat und Religion, Judentum und Christentum," in *Jüdische Schriften,* Vol. III (1924).

Dunin-Borkowski, Stanislaus, Graf von: *Randglossen zu Spinozas Schrift über die Freiheit des Philosophierens.* No place, no publisher, 1910.

——: *Spinoza.* 4 vols. Münster, Aschendorff, 1933–6.

Erdmann, J. E.: "Spinoza," in *Versuch einer wissenschaftlichen Darstellung der Geschichte der neueren Philosophie.* 7 vols. (Facsimile of 1834–42 ed.) Stuttgart, Frommann, 1933.

Fischer, Kuno: *Spinozas Leben, Werke und Lehre.* 5th ed. Heidelberg, C. Winter, 1919.

Freudenthal, Jacob: *Die Lebensgeschichte Spinoza's in Quellenschriften, Urkunden und nichtamtlichen Nachrichten.* Leipzig, Veit, 1899.

——: *Spinoza, Leben und Lehre.* Heidelberg, C. Winter, 1927.

*Froude, J. A.: "Spinoza," in *Short Studies on Great Subjects.* First Series. 3d ed. London, Longmans, Green, 1868.

Grunwald, Max: *Spinoza in Deutschland.* Berlin, S. Calvary, 1897.

*Hampshire, Stuart: *Spinoza.* Harmondsworth, Middlesex, Penguin Books, 1951.

*——: "Spinoza and the Idea of Freedom," in British Academy (London), *Proceedings,* XLVI (1960), 195–215.

*McKeon, Richard: *The Philosophy of Spinoza: The Unity of His Thought.* New York, Longmans, Green, 1928.

*Pollock, Sir Frederick: *Spinoza: His Life and Philosophy.* 2d ed. London, Duckworth; New York, Macmillan, 1899. 2d ed., corr. and reissued, London, Duckworth, 1912.

*Roth, Leon: *Spinoza, Descartes and Maimonides.* Oxford, 1924; New York, Russell & Russell, 1963.

*——: *Spinoza.* London, Allen & Unwin, 1954.

Sérouya, Henri: *Spinoza, sa vie, sa philosophie.* New ed., rev. & augm. Paris, A. Michel, 1947.

Strauss, Leo: *Die Religionskritik Spinozas als Grundlage seiner Bibelwissenschaft.* Berlin, Akademie-Verlag, 1930.

Vernière, Paul: *Spinoza et la pensée française avant la Révolution.* Paris, Presses Universitaires de France, 1954.

*Wolf, Abraham: *Spinoza, Benedictus de: Short Treatise on God, Man and His Well-Being,* trans. and ed. with introduction, commentary and a life of Spinoza by Abraham Wolf. London, A. & C. Black, 1910.

*Wolfson, Harry Austryn: *The Philosophy of Spinoza.* 2 vols. Cambridge, Harvard University Press, 1934; 2 vols. in 1, New York, Meridian Books, 1960.

*——: *Spinoza: A Life of Reason.* New York, Modern Classics, 1932.

INDEX OF NAMES